WALLS of GLASS

A Survival Guide for Families in the Ministry

Dr. Russell Glenn Riggs

Printed in the United States of America
Cover and text design by the Aslan Group • Baton Rouge, LA

All scripture quotations are from the King James Version of the Bible. For clarity, all scripture is in italics with the reference. Any deviations from the King James Bible are not intentional.

ISBN 0-9706083-0-6

For more information:
Soldiers of the Cross Publications
115 North Christiana Avenue
Apopka, Florida 32704
(407) 884-8811

"Uneasy lies the head that wears a crown"

—Shakespeare

Dedication

This book is dedicated to my family...Dr. Glenn Riggs, Dr. Carolyn Riggs, Rev. Samuel Riggs, Dr. Daniel Riggs, Mrs. Christy Carringer, Miss Cindy Riggs, and my dear wife, Christy and our daughter Savannah.

Though our ship has gone through many storms, it just keeps on sailing.

I love you all!

—Rusty

Special Thanks:

To Teresa Marcus for all her work on typing this book.

To Howard Marcus for his help in art design.

To Tommy and Lori Ray of The Aslan Group for the great job on the cover.

To Dr. Bill Grady for coaching me through my first book.

To Dr. Johnny Pope for his work on the forward.

To all the P.K.'s who inspired this book.

To my Lord and Saviour Jesus Christ for saving my soul and using me in His royal service.

To my wife for her help in proof reading and being patient with me during all the hours I dedicated to writing.

To my family for allowing me to write about candid moments.

We Are Soldiers of the Cross

Onward Christian soldiers, off to war we go,
Get up, Christian soldiers, it's time to face the foe.

We're in the battle of the Ages between wrong and right,
To lead desperate souls from darkness and into the saving Light.

We are called to go to war with battles that go unseen
To redeem the very souls of men and to keep our country clean.

Our enemy has fought us hard and he'll win at any cost,
He's destroyed the lives of many and he loves to keep them lost.

He's out there waiting and planning hard to over throw our Lord,
He's out there waiting, working hard while sowing his discord.

He cares for none, he kills and lies while hate's his only creed.
Yet still, his force has grown so strong, with many to follow his lead.

So come on my fellow warriors, pick up your sword to fight!
These's someone out there who's lost and weary, who needs to find the light

Someday, the viscous war shall end and we'll see the Master face to face,
He'll say, "Well done good and faithful, you've won the good hard race."

"Come and lay down your bloody sword, for with me you will forever dwell,
I've bound your enemy that old devil up and cast him into Hell!'"

But until then we must keep fighting and endure our every loss,
And never let it be forgotten we are Soldiers of the Cross!

—Russell G. Riggs

Reviews

"*Walls of Glass* is a tremendously insightful discussion of what it means to be a preacher's kid. I wish every preacher's kid in America would be given a copy and would study it carefully. There is a lot in *Walls of Glass* for the parents of preacher's kids as well."

Dr. Phil Stringer, Executive Vice President
Landmark Baptist College, Haines City, FL

"*Walls of Glass* is a rich, interesting, and exciting story of God's saving grace. It is the account of a man called of God to the greatest work in the world—the preaching of the gospel. The author successfully opens our minds to the weakness of the flesh and the power of God to make us victorious Christians. *Walls of Glass* is good reading for Christians young and old.

Dr. Lee Roberson, Founder and Chancellor
Tennessee Temple University Chattanooga, TN

"I hope you enjoy Dr. Russell Riggs' book *Walls of Glass.* Rusty is the son of my dear friend Glenn Riggs and I have known him since he was a little boy. It is a blessing to see him grow up and continue to serve our Lord and Savior Jesus Christ. We think that you will find many useful items in his book and we do hope it will be helpful to you in your Christian walk with God.

Jim Vineyard, Pastor
Windsor Hills Baptist Church
Oklahoma Baptist College, Oklahoma City, OK

"I laughed and cried as I read *Walls of Glass.* I grew up in a very busy and successful pastor's home and have been my dad's associate pastor now for twenty-eight years. What a blessing and help this book will be to pastor's children."

Steve Roberson, Co Pastor
Gospel Light Baptist Church Walkertown, NC

Table of Contents

Foreword
Introduction

1. The Adventure Begins 1
2. Harsh Realities of Being a P.K. 19
3. Helpful Hints 49
4. Things I've Found 84
5. Is It Really That Bad? 91
6. Dangerous Attitudes 96
7. Why Do So Many Go Bad? 111
8. Don't Just Take My Word For It 117
9. Raising a Minister's Kid 125

Epilogue

FOREWORD

I just finished reading the manuscript of *Walls of Glass* by Dr. Russell G. Riggs. When Rusty asked me to write the forward, I was touched. I have to admit we in the ministry sometimes overlook what God is doing in the lives of our own kids! I have known Rusty since he was a little boy, he, like so many preacher's children, even our own, make up the background in the tapestry of the life and ministry God has given to us. I had every intention of reading as fast as I could to say, "Okay, Rusty, I've read it . . .now here's your forward." However, while reading *Walls of Glass,* I kept slowing down to meditate upon the wisdom God has given this young man, wisdom beyond his years; wisdom from God!

I see in Rusty Riggs, a flagship for our next generation. He, and God willing, others in his generation are moving from the background of the tapestry to the foreground in deep and brilliant colors of conviction and dedication to our Lord and Saviour, Jesus Christ!

You will enjoy this book whether you are a preacher's kid, preacher, deacon's kid, deacon, or lay person. It is a book that will challenge adults to practice what we preach. Rusty impressed me with how important little things are and how observant children are to our actions and reactions of the parents they respect. He also stressed the importance of accountability for youth to make the right decisions.

This book had me wanting to laugh, cry, or say Amen throughout the reading. I couldn't put it down!

May the Lord's richest blessing rest upon Rusty, his wife and young family! It has been a joy to be friends and minister with his dad, Dr. Glenn Riggs, a truly great preacher. It is obvious to me that the mantle of blessing has been successfully passed. As I came to the end of the book, I had this knowledge in my heart that we haven't heard the last from Rusty Riggs.

God's speed Rusty, and may the Lord increase your tribe.

—Dr. Johnny Pope

Introduction

Hi, allow me to introduce myself. I'm Russell G. Riggs. My friends call me Rusty. My middle name was given to me in honor of my dad, Pastor Glenn Riggs. Yes, I said Pastor. I'm one of those bratty P.K.'s that everybody knows. That little child running around the church who always seemed to find trouble no matter how hard I tried to run from it. I had hundreds of "parents" or informers to keep me from getting away with all the things the other kids (including their kids) did.

Somehow I survived all the tattling, constructive criticism, hypocrisy, pride swallowing, pressure, responsibilities, cutthroats, backstabbers, loss of friends, moving, new schools, new teachers, new homes, new churches, competition, seeing the heroes with feet of clay, seeing burned out Christians, feeling burned out, seeing my parents attacked by people with a third of the character, two faced people, being in big churches, in small churches, hearing the ever popular "the pastor's kid did it" or the great "you're supposed to be different because you're the pastor's kid". By the grace of God I made it through it all and now I can honestly say I'm proud to be a pastor's kid!

Over the years I've been saddened by the number of "P.K.'s" that I've met with similar stories, who have been beaten by the harsh life that is being the child of a minister. I've met many who have allowed the hard knocks to disillusion them with the life that God chose for them. There are an alarming number of pastor's children who no longer serve God, or have a burden for people or even go to church. This news is, however, not surprising. It's hard to live a life when you feel everyone has an opinion of you and your family. It's a life where everything you do, say, and go is open for scrutiny in the public eye. I've thought many times that I and my family lived in a house with walls made of transparent glass, open for all to see and discuss.

Does this story sound familiar? Then, you must read the rest of this book. We are in this situation together. The life you have is hard, but it's not impossible.

It can actually be filled with many joys, if you can learn to make the necessary adjustments and get the right frame of mind! Let me share my life story with you, just to show you that we all are in the same boat. Most "P.K.'s" lead similar lives, and if you have been chosen to perform this task, then you need to be prepared or Satan will sift you like wheat. In the following pages you will hear my story, my brother's and sister's, as well as several other pastor's kids who survived their life in the glass house.

> *"Nature is upheld by antagonism. Passions, resistance, danger are educators. We acquire the strength we have overcome."*
>
> —Emerson

"Nobody conquers until he fights."

—Dr. Jack Hyles

Epilogue

I hope that this book has been and will be a help to you and your family. I don't claim to be perfect or even above the problems that plague the families of ministers. I've got my deep scars and occasionally sadness sweeps my mind as I reflect over the years, but over all it's been good! I don't know all the problems but I do know the answer is always Jesus!

If you've read this book it's possible that you are searching your soul for answers. If you have never received Jesus as your Saviour then I beg you to consider doing it today! You will never be satisfied or know true joy without Jesus as your personal Saviour. Ask him into your heart today!!

I wish you peace. I wish you joy. May the sun shine always on your face and may the wind blow gently on your back. I have a good life, a good family name, and a beautiful wife and child. May God grant you the joy he's already given to me.

Sincerely,
Russell G. Riggs, Ph.D.

For information on copies of this book or to book the author for revivals, youth camps, conferences or meetings,write or call:

Dr. Russell G. Riggs
820 Rolling Green Dr.
Apopka, FL 32703

(407) 884-8811

1
The Adventure Begins

In a suburb of St. Louis, a tall, slim, farm boy with Michael Landonish looks, and dreams of rock and roll stardom, came to know the Lord. Glenn Riggs was a southern boy who grew up on a farm in Northeast Arkansas but moved to St. Louis to find a better life.

He married his high school sweetheart, a pastor's daughter named Carolyn, who resembled a Hollywood starlet with her blond flowing hair, green eyes, and sense of style that made her the dream of more than one farm boy.

Although Dad was raised in a very moral and good home, he didn't get saved until he was nineteen after following my mother's example to walk down the aisle and receive Christ. Soon after, God captured his heart, his life, and his future. He was as they say, "on fire for God". The call to preach was inevitable, and soon Dad yielded to the onslaught of conviction that was poured upon him.

While in St. Louis, my parents gave birth to my sister Christy. They were real active in their church. They learned to go soul winning and to teach Sunday School, but soon Dad realized that the call to preach is a call to prepare. So, he, my mother, and my sister packed up and moved to Bible college.

In a small Northeast Arkansas town called Walnut Ridge lay the campus of Williams Baptist College. It was here that my life began. My mother gave birth to me on the early summer morning of August 26th, 1970. My dad was a student preacher who was already pastoring a country church. I entered this world with the label of being a pastor's kid. It was all I knew or would ever know.

My dad completed his college there and the Lord moved my parents to another town in Arkansas called Hot Springs. The church was Grand Avenue Baptist Church and it was here that the earliest memories of my life took place.

I can remember the small red brick parsonage there. It was a pretty house with a rose bush growing in front. By this time my parents had given birth to my two younger brothers, Samuel and Daniel, twins who were born premature but God had seen them through it and they were healthy, cute little fellows who would accompany me on many adventures. The parsonage was a three bedroom red brick home that was built in what used to be a nice neighborhood but it had the misfortune of low cost housing being built around it which brought in many undesirable people and the crime that seems to follow with them. Our house was robbed and broken into several times while we lived there. Bikes, big wheels, toys, things like these were stolen by the neighborhood kids and teenagers.

My dad by this time was an upcoming young pastor with a very busy schedule which called on him to be gone for days at a time, preaching in revivals and conferences all around the South. I remember many times when I'd be scared at night because my dad would be gone and I was afraid we'd be robbed. The church put up a big fence around the house to serve two purposes, one, to help ward off criminals and, two, to keep us kids from escaping from the yard and getting out in the street.

The church dad was pastoring was booming. In just a few short years, it grew from one hundred to six hundred in Sunday School. The church was so excited! I was a small boy but I can still remember those Vacation Bible Schools and big days at church. I remember one day, it was Old fashioned Day and Mother had bought me some old fashioned overalls like the ones my

Grandpa wore. I was so excited, but I wanted my hair cut. Mother was busy cooking food all day Saturday for the big dinner on the grounds, so I decided to take matters into my own hands. I got the scissors out and did a butcher, hack job on my wavy blonde hair. When my mother found me, all she could do was cry. It was an old fashioned day that I'll never forget!

Things were going so well at church. It was growing and they were leading in the state of Arkansas in baptisms as well as being noted for such tremendous growth. It seemed every Sunday I saw someone saved and baptized. The church built a gymnasium and started a Christian school and made plans to build a 2,000 seat auditorium in the future.

I can still remember some of the blessings of being the pastor's kid. There was this man, I don't even remember his name, but every Sunday when I'd shake his hand, he'd give me a pack of Dentyne chewing gum and say, "How's my pastor's boy doing?", or "How's my preacher boy today?" I'd smack the gum all through church until my mother would make me spit it out. There was another man who'd give my brothers, sister, and I a small candy bar most every Sunday. There was a lady who'd often make cookies or cakes for us. We were "in the zone" as they say. We thought it was as good as it could get.

Just as we thought we had it all, Satan got into the mix and took notice of the great work going on there. You see, the growth of this church brought conversions of many African-American people or black people as we called them then. This church had a segment of people from the Old South who did not want their church "polluted" with inferior people who didn't look like them. They began to grumble and complain about how this pastor was ruining their church.

They got together and tried to fire dad, but the church had grown so much with dad, they couldn't get enough people on their side to accomplish the coup d'etat. These conspirators were men of influence, deacons, rich business men, and pillars of the church. They decided other means to try to dispose of this unwanted preacher. They began to attack. It's funny, though, they were a little afraid to attack the pastor directly, so they did the next best thing. They attacked his wife and kids. My mother took most of the abuse. It's amazing how mean people can be.

I was in the nursery, a young three year old boy when I began to come home with bruises that were unexplainable. One Sunday I came home with a huge bump on my head. The nursery director said that I fell down and bumped my head. It seemed like a logical explanation, so my parents dismissed it, knowing that I was a busy little fellow who played wide open, a thousand miles a minute. It was about a week later when a teenage girl who was helping in the nursery came in to see my mother, crying. She told my mother how she could no longer be silent and that I'd been being abused by the nursery director (who was the wife of one of the deacons trying to expel dad). She had spanked me real hard for no real reason, and once when I was crying, she picked me up and threw me into a rocking chair from several feet away. The chair flipped over and I knocked my head on the floor. At an early age I'd already become wise to the evils of church politics.

Things began to get edgy as this battle began to boil. This group of inner people were determined to take control of their church again and return it to it's small all white congregation. They decided the next step was to starve us out. They voted to cut dad's pay and then right before Christmas they decided, without warning, to do away with the Christmas bonus that my parents depended on to buy their four little kids Christmas. I understood later my parents got lucky with being approved for a Sears card a few days before Christmas where they charged all of our toys for Christmas.

My parents saw that they were fighting a losing battle. These people were determined to win even if it meant destroying the church and my family to do it. Dad's job finally came up for a public church vote, the church overwhelmingly voted down the deacons. It was a bittersweet victory. Dad won but the church lost and the good sweet spirit was forever damaged.

In 1976 my parents resigned and the Lord moved us to another Arkansas town called Rodgers. There the Open Door Baptist Church was our new home.

We were there for about one year. I went to a new school. I didn't really understand what happened. I just knew that everything changed. I missed my house, friends, and the school I had attended for Kindergarten.

Everything was new. I was afraid to sleep in my new room, it was strange to me. My brothers and I shared a room. I slept on the top bunk and my twin brothers had their own beds but they would usually at some point end up in bed together as they were used to never being apart. We never really adjusted to Rodgers. It never felt like home. Somehow I knew, even as a little six year old boy that our life would not be there for long. About the time I started getting used to it and making new friends, we moved again.

A small group of nineteen people had written and called dad asking him to come back to Hot Springs and start an independent, fundamental, Baptist church. So, in August of 1977, my family again loaded a big U-haul and returned to the town that had been so hard on us before. I guess it's true when the Bible says that God works in mysterious ways!

That fall my parents and my dad's music director, Dr. Glenn Lewis started the Great Hot Springs Baptist Temple in the back of Kilby's Restaurant. In a small banquet room a great church was birthed.

It was so exciting. I was seven years old now and was still too young to know what was happening, but it was neat! The church grew so quickly. We bought an old Nazarene church building in downtown Hot Springs. It was an hundred year old rock building with a bell tower and a balcony that creaked when you walked in it. It was a scary place to me, but it was my new church. It was with this church that I spent most of my childhood and my mind is so full of memories, both bitter and sweet.

Hot Springs Baptist Temple soon became the fastest growing

church in the state of Arkansas and among the elite churches of the nation.

Dad's ministry was now bigger than ever. Churches all around America wanted him to come for revivals and bus conferences, youth conferences, church camps, and church growth conferences. We began to see our dad very little as he would be gone three and four weeks in a normal month. He would fly in Saturday morning and he would go to visitation all day Saturday, preach on Sunday, and I would go to school on Monday and he was usually headed to an airport to go out of town.

It became a treat to get to see dad and spend time with him. My mother had a hard time raising four kids and by 1980 my youngest sister, Cindy, was born in the middle of this madness. Mother was alone for most of the eight years we were there!

I don't want you to get me wrong, with everything there's good and bad. We enjoyed the perks that accompanied success. Dad was a local celebrity. I went to a youth conference one year. A teenage boy came up to me and said, "Aren't you Rusty Riggs?" I said, "Yes." He said, "Wow, your dad is my hero." I was so proud at that moment. My brothers and sister were at times treated like royalty. I was even asked to autograph Bibles from time to time! There were many people who were good to us and my parents. I always try to never forget that!

Churches sometimes change over time. This church quickly went from being the humble new church with nineteen people who were good people that worked hard and had humility to a church with 2,200 people with a multi-million dollar facility, a large Christian school, a college, lots of notoriety, and influence. Dad was chosen as the President of the Arkansas Christian School Association during this time (1979-1985). He served the state diligently as a lobbyist for the A.C.S.A. This meant trips to Washington every year and more speaking engagements. This required dad to be away from his home and his church more than ever. I remember a bill was presented that proposed a great danger to the Christian school movement.

This threw dad into countless hours of overtime lobbying and rallies. We finally won that battle. As we celebrated our victory, another battle was brewing. This time it was a powerful law firm in Little Rock and a powerful Attorney General picking up the sword and declaring war against this Christian school movement.

The Christian Law Association and Attorney David Gibbs were called in and for almost one year every day dad was getting up at four or five o'clock in the morning to drive one and a half hours to the Little Rock Courthouse to go to battle. It was a southern David and Goliath battle to the end. We finally won the lawsuit, but by the time it was over that Attorney General was then the Governor of Arkansas, Dr. Gibbs health was failing him, Dad was exhausted and pushed to the limit, returning to a church that was somehow changed and would never be the same again. We had gotten used to the hard driving light of battle. We had seen the news crews on the lawn, 60 Minutes anchorman calling for interviews with this country preacher that I called Dad, countless newspaper articles and a head to head battle with the Governor of Arkansas. By the way, that law firm was the now infamous Rose Law Firm with Hillary Clinton and that Attorney General was a young man from Hot Springs, Arkansas named Bill Clinton.

When all the dust settled dad returned to his normal life but things, as I've stated already, were different. The long hours had taken their toll. Dad's health was bad, he'd lost a lot of weight and had developed a health problem during the middle of this. He'd come home and wasn't the joyful, happy, playful dad we knew before. He'd eat dinner then tackle the stacks of files and books of law, not to mention the duties that accompany running a church of 2,200 members, a Christian school, and a Bible college.

Somewhere in all this his family was lost. Don't get me wrong, Dad was a good dad, and loved his kids dearly, but it was God's work. His wife and kids should not stand in the way of God's work, others needed dad more than we did, right? Wrong, this finally took it's toll on us.

Mother's life had been wrapped up in us kids. But we were rapidly growing up and now entering teenhood. Mother saw her life would soon come to an end. Mom and Dad had not been able to work on things at home, we had almost become strangers to him and that's hard. We felt like we couldn't compete with God and felt wrong to attempt to do so. As dad was busy helping to build all the church families, his own began to crumble.

Out of respect for my parents, all I will say on this matter is that they had some marriage problems. It was for a brief time, but separation was frightfully close to entering our home. My parents had character, though. They worked it out and got Christian counseling. Today, they are like newlyweds most of the time (much to the embarrassment of their teenage children - parents aren't supposed to be mushy, right?).

Word of the marriage problems leaked out into the church. Some in the church didn't understand how this could happen nor were they nearly as forgiving as we'd hoped. These folks took a real harsh stance and when they heard that the counselor told dad to take a lot of time off and be with mother, they wouldn't have it. Choose your wife and kids or us was the general attitude. I remember the pain and betrayal we all felt as long time friends turned on us, many people dad had baptized and led to Christ. He'd married them and spent hours helping them through their personal crisis including many marriage problems. As a fourteen year old boy, I remember seeing the empire crumble around us as it was very evident that us kids and mom were unwanted and expendable. I must say, though, the majority of the church was loyal and loved their pastor. It was, again, a small but powerful inner group that had a problem. Most of those people have since apologized and expressed regret.

I went to school and heard horrible things said by some of the other kids about my parents. I sat through horrible business meetings and saw some of dad's staff turn on him. My coach began to bench me and I had been his leading scorer all year. He began to yell at me and do all he could to make my life miserable. I became angry and bitter, a kid just trying to make it through teenhood. I couldn't understand why this was happening.

My sister and I went from being popular and liked to being shunned. Everyone would go out to parties or running around but we were no longer welcomed. We found ourselves just hanging on to each other to get through it until the end of the school year. I thank God for my brothers and sister, they were my shelter during many storms.

It came as no surprise when dad announced to us that God was moving us in May of 1985, but the next location was a shock. Dad and Mom decided to enter the mission field and we were packing up and moving to, of all places, Honolulu, Hawaii !! We kids were shocked, but excited. I'd seen Hawaii Five-O and Magnum, P.I. I was thinking to myself about beaches and mountains, beautiful Hawaiian women. We were moving to paradise. It was going to be a dream life.

Then came a reality check! Suddenly, I was auctioning off my toys and bed and my motorcycle. We couldn't take it with us, so it had to be sold to cover the costs of moving to this expensive place. I remember I had to give my dogs away. I had raised my beagles since they were pups. I named one Smith and the other Wesson. They were rabbit hunting dogs. Smith died that summer but I had to give Wesson to a good friend. That was hard. I also said goodbye to my friends, Philip Graham and Jensen Peyte, good friends who'd been loyal to me. I stood at an airport on August 28, 1985 and told my grandparents and cousins and aunts and uncles and my best friends a tearful goodbye. I felt such pain as I wondered if I'd ever see them again. Some of them I won't see again until I join them in heaven.

I was a southern boy headed to a life that was absolutely different in every way than I'd ever seen. Hawaii was in many ways the best and worst times of my life!

After moving there, we began the adjustment period. I became very angry and bitter for a period. I couldn't understand what God was doing. I became a little rebellious and took my anger out on my parents who were still trying amidst all these changes to fix their improving marriage.

We started the Windward Baptist Temple in Kailua, Hawaii in a public school cafeteria. I became suddenly an important person to my dad. No longer did dad have twenty two full time staff members to depend on. For the first time dad actually needed me as his helper with the Lord's work. It was in this church that I developed my love for God's work and learned what it was to have a pastor's heart. I was actually a part of the church work. It wasn't any longer just my dad's church. We all had a part in building that church. God was so good to us during those years and I saw the ever protective hand of God on our lives.

I saw things I thought didn't really exist. I saw witchcraft, demon possession, and occult activity of the islands which really opened my eyes to the spiritual warfare talked about in Ephesians six. I also saw God work and do great things, miracles. We truly lived by faith and God never once let us down!

I remember times when we were at our last dime and a check would come out of nowhere and be just enough to get us through another month. We worked with several military bases and had sailors from Pearl Harbor, fly boys from Hickam Air Force Base, marines from the Kaneohe Marine Corps Air Station and army g.i.s from Red Hill. It was awesome to touch the lives of these young men. They were lonely, scared, and for the first time on their own.

I remember onall the holidays our house would be full of military men and ladies and we touched their life and gave them a piece of home in this land that was so different from the farms and neighborhoods of mainland U.S.A. Eighteen of these young men entered the ministry and two young Hawaiian boys entered the ministry who now pastor churches in Hawaii. We left a little bit of ourselves forever embedded in that beautiful Hawaiian island.

I'll never forget the sorrowful day when we announced to the church that it was time for us to go back to the mainland. There were so many lives, both locals and military that loved us and didn't want us to go back. It was God's timing and we knew that

God wanted us to return home. I'll also never forget the grown, big Hawaiian men as they hugged us and cried like a baby. I'll also never forget a man named Casey Boyet who was such a help to me through my high school years and taught me so much through athletics and love. I loved those people and I think of them often.

We made plans to go from Hawaii to Orlando, Florida to start a church. I had graduated from high school and had won a scholarship at Oklahoma Baptist College playing basketball. So, my family made plans to move to Orlando and I made plans to attend O.B.C. and prepare to enter my own ministry as a preacher. I had surrendered to preach at eleven years old and was now excited to spread my wings and take the world by storm! As every eighteen year old I was invincible and cocky.

I left on my eighteenth birthday to go to college and told my parents goodbye for six months as I went to conquer the world. I found out the first night as I cried on my pillow that my family was more important to me than ever. I wanted to go home after the first day!

I stuck it out and actually began to like the fast paced life of college and college basketball. I'll always praise the Lord for the ministry of Dr. Jim Vineyard who helped me and my family out more than he'll ever know. I'll also never forget how God sent Dr. Russell Anderson and his wife into our lives in Hawaii to be a good friend and source of strength. These two men will never know how much I love them.

Well, anyway, back to my story. I came home for Christmas break. I couldn't believe how much I missed my family! My brothers had grown from five foot five inches to six foot three inches in six months! My mother's cooking had never tasted so good nor had my dad's embrace felt so welcomed. During this break dad asked me to take one semester off and help them in January move from Jonesboro, Arkansas to Orlando, Florida. I was happy at college but I knew dad needed me. I couldn't turn my back on the ones who'd always been there for me and worked so hard to raise me. So, I decided to move to Orlando for one semester and help my parents get the church started.

Once again we pulled up a big U-haul truck and loaded our whole life into boxes and packed it all into that big truck and we formed a caravan with our good friend Bro. Larry Stephens driving the truck and all of us following in our cars all the way to the city beautiful, Orlando, Florida.

We were excited to be back in action after a six month layover in Arkansas. My dad always started churches with no financial support. He sold vinyl siding to help him support his family while starting the church. He was ready to get back into the pulpit and we were ready to help. Being back in the South would be so much easier as the culture difference would be abolished.

One of the things that was hard about the church in Hawaii was that all of our peers were back in the mainland. We were used to men like Johnny Pope, Bob Gray, Jack Hyles, Lee Roberson, Carl Hatch, Jim Vineyard, Dave Gibbs, Tom Malone, Dave Hyles, Dennis Corle, Steve Roberson, Howard Hall, and John Bishop. All those great preachers were regular guests in our church and home. I missed the excitement that they brought with them. In Hawaii we felt isolated often and most of our peers were not around.

When we came back to the mainland the year was 1988. A lot of things had changed during the years we were gone. There was battling and rifts in fundamentalism. Many of our heroes were no longer able to share pulpits. There was now, it seemed, a blacklist of preachers. I remember being saddened when I realized that my dad was, it seemed, on that list. Rumors spread about our family. It was said that Dr. Glenn Riggs was a has been and that he'd been out of the ministry vacationing in Hawaii ! He'd become a caution tale. I and my family were deeply hurt by some of the men who used to be our friends. I remember when dad pastored the big church and was "The Man". He preached for all of them and they preached for him. Now they wouldn't touch us with a ten foot pole.

I remember thinking how unfair this was, we were the same people we were then, or maybe we weren't! We no longer had anything to offer as a retainer for their friendship. They no longer had anything to gain from knowing the Riggs family.

For a while, as a pastor's kid and a young preacher boy this really bothered me and my siblings. We knew our dad had the right stuff and belonged with the "Big Guns" of fundamentalism. Now I understand some things. These men that hurt us, (whose names I'll not mention, I'm not seeking revenge, just trying to help those of you who have gone through this!), are human like anybody else. They make human mistakes and it wasn't really anything that my family did, rather it was their insecurity and need to feel important. Kicking a man who was down was something that made them somehow feel bigger, like a bully on a playground. Many pastors are great preachers, their just poor friends. My dad taught me a valuable lesson. He chose his wife and watching his kids grow up over the thrills of being a big name. His example is something I hope to emulate myself. Many of the big guys have paid a big price for their celebrity. For many of them they gained the world and lost their own family.

I learned that I'd rather be fishing with my dad or hunting for deer than to see his name in lights. Many P.K.'s see their dad in many pulpits, but not at the dinner table. A false balance is an abomination and many preachers are out of balance when it comes to their home and their ministry.

We went on anyway and dad now forty years old decided to start the Starlight Baptist Church. Our seventh church and the third one to start from scratch. We turned our attention from the problems of fundamentalism and put all of our attention on this baby church. God sent us some dear old friends, the Crigger and Stephens families to assist us. I was nineteen years old now. I was planning to get back to school at Oklahoma Baptist College in August when dad came to me and asked me if I would pray about staying home and helping him start the church and become the youth pastor of Starlight while getting my education at a local Bible college. After praying about it I decided to do it.

Again, God blessed our family with an exciting church. Starlight started in the back of a square dance hall in Longwood, Florida. We used to tell people to bring two pair of shoes to church to make fun of the fact that our church was in a dance hall. The church grew incredibly fast. In fact, it was growing so well it made my head spin. We went from nineteen to about five hundred in two years! We broke the 1,000 mark three times before the second anniversary and we started a Christian school during our third year. Starlight Baptist Church was chosen and awarded the prestigious "Fastest growing church in America" honors for 1992. We were back in the saddle again! My youth department which was my pride and joy grew from two to four average attendance to eighty then to one hundred average attendance. I was so proud of it but scared of it all at the same time. If history had taught me anything, it taught me that when everything is perfect, Satan would soon appear and appear he did.

In the fall of our third year we began to experience some growing pains. There were people in the church who'd moved their membership to our church. They loved the way dad preached, they just didn't like what he preached. It was apparent that our old fashioned, hell fire, separation was more than many of them could handle. They did the usual, get together to discuss the pastor and his family over coffee and doughnuts. Reports of griping began to circulate. By the time it all hit the fan, there was a rebellion started. Unfortunately dad's music director bought into all of it. He thought he was the leader and that it was up to him to "fix" our church.

He came up with several accusations which were all proven undoubtedly false. When he realized that he was mistaken, he knew that he'd showed himself as a disloyal staff member. He resigned and he started a movement with several of his disgruntled followers to split and start his own church.

They tried everything to run my family off. They tried to legally take our building away which was shot down by our bank's lawyers. They tried slander, implications, lies, accusations. Every week we'd hear a new story, but we ignored it and kept on doing God's work.

After several months of sweating it out, the Music Director, Sunday School Superintendent, and the Adult Class Sunday School Teacher, got together and started their own church and took about thirty people with them.

They sent letters to every member of our church and stated all the things in which they disagreed with Pastor Riggs and invited them to come to their church. For the most part, they didn't get any more people, but unfortunately, they got the wealthiest people to go with them.

They started a church which had three pastors or elders and they had the motto, "a church ran by the people for the people". It lasted about three months and split three ways, each "pastor" taking some of the people.

Now a small remnant meets with about twenty people led by the high and mighty Music Director.

The effects of the split back at Starlight were felt in several ways. Loss of friends, good people caught in the middle who refused to take sides so they left and went to other churches. We also lost momentum. Dad was very discouraged by this. Our church lost a lot members over the next six months. Not only did we lose people to the split, but the recession of 1991-92 caused many of our members to move up north to get work. Every week we said goodbye to another good family and friend.

The worst part about it for me was the fact that I was engaged to a girl whose parents left during the split. Her dad was our Sunday School Superintendent and became one of the three pastors of the split church. He vowed to break us up and her mom said that we'll never allow you to marry our daughter. It took them about two months to break us up, but they finally succeeded.

My brother Danny also lost his girlfriend to the split as her family was related to the Music Director and left with him. Danny and I were hurt and confused as to why the Lord allowed this to happen. It took me a while to get over the pain of this loss. I grew closer to God through it and I now praise God that He had His protective hand over me and kept me from making a huge mistake and marrying out of His will.

All through this experience dad told us kids to ignore the opportunity to fight or defend ourselves. I used to get so frustrated by this. Mom and Dad said to let God handle it. Then, I didn't understand it but now that I've grown and become a little wiser, I see that by staying in God's will we stayed in his protection and those people did us a favor in the long run. God had seen us through and Starlight survived it and became even stronger because of it! They meant it for harm but God used it for good. So many good people stayed by our side and were truly loyal. I don't care what anybody says, the best people I have met, I have met in church!

I continued to work at Starlight for about four more years. We grew and continued to break our own records and are now a very strong and solid church. I had a wonderful time as both the pastor's son and the Assistant Pastor. I was able to learn so many valuable lessons on working with people under my dad's watchful eye and guiding hand. Starlight allowed me to make "preacher boy" mistakes. The church put up with my constant pushing and childish energy. I did such no-no's as taking a group of teenage boys to toilet paper the cars of staff members in the dark of night and soaping the water fountains of the rich well-to-do neighborhoods of our city. Dad would give me the lectures on how it would look to the church if his son and their Youth Pastor was arrested for such childish behavior. What can I say? I was much younger then.

I knew I was loved by most of the people at dad's church, sure there were those who thought I was spoiled or a punk who was handed everything but they were few. I found out on September 19, 1995 at 15 till 3:00 p.m. just how much people did love me and respect me. I was in a terrible motorcycle accident which left me almost dead! I had two broken arms, a fractured hip, severe leg damage and was paralyzed for two months from the waist down. They airlifted me to the Orlando Regency Hospital where I fought for my life for several days. As the news spread, over four hundred people came to the hospital and most of them stayed in the lobbies until I was stabilized. They prayed nonstop for me. I know God heard them because I somehow made it through that personal disaster.

I received over five hundred get well cards. There were so many visitors the hospital thought I was a V.I.P. or a star. They wondered who in the world I was. They were shocked to find I was just a pastor's kid from Winter Springs. So many Christians from around America sent letters and cards. Who says being a pastor's kid doesn't come with rewards! I loved those people and those teenagers very much. I was able to teach them and I also learned a lot from them in return. As I look back now I see just how patient and forgiving the church was with me. They saw me through my reckless teen years and my never ending (it seemed) date life, all the way to adulthood.

I left Starlight in 1996 to become the Pastor of a brand new church in Apopka, Florida called Apopka Baptist Temple. It was only three months old when I went there. When I resigned at Starlight it was with much pain and reservation but I knew God wanted me in Apopka. The church was sad and there were many tears and hugs on my last Sunday at Starlight Baptist Church. Now I was on to a totally new experience, no longer was I the pastor's kid, I was the Pastor.

As I look back and reflect I see how God used each and every person and problem to mold me and make me better. Someone wrote once "what doesn't kill us makes us stronger". To that I say "Amen"! I saw so many great things, I met so many great men of God and had the privilege of knowing personally men like Dr. Lee Roberson, Dr. Jack Hyles, Dr. Robert Gray, Dr. Carl Hatch, Dr. Johnny Pope, Dr. Mickey Carter, Dr. Jim Vineyard, Dr. Russell Anderson, Dr. Bill Grady, and the list goes on and on. I love pastors, pastors of great churches, and pastors of rural churches like my papaw, Rev. Jack Booth, who pastored for forty years in small towns in Michigan and Arkansas. I can honestly say that there have been bad times but the good has far outweighed the bad. I've thanked God often for allowing me the honor of being a pastor's kid. I would not have had it any other way! God chose me to be in this very special position.

Now, you say Rusty why have you bored us with this long drawn out history lesson? I believe that for you to continue reading this book with the intent to be helped and encouraged it's essential for you to see me as one who's felt the warm sunshine of the mountain tops but also as one who's been in the smothering, lonely valleys along the way. I know the good and the bad that accompanies life behind walls of glass and I survived it and so can you.

In the pages to come I will systematically lay out the dangers and pitfalls of being a child of a minister. The life you have is one that must be lived circumspectly and soberly. There are things you must do and things you must not do. I hope that you will continue to read on and may you find the words to be both enlightening and encouraging.

I don't claim in this book or in my life to have attained perfection as a preacher's kid. William Shakespeare once wrote, " The fool doth think he is wise, but the wise man doth know himself to be a fool." God knows I've made my share of mistakes! (What are they? None of your business!) I'm just a guy who did the best he could and made the most of it to enjoy the life that God made me for! As I teach, I am continually being taught. Now read on for more instruction.

"A wise man will hear, and will increase learning; and a man of understanding shall attain unto wise counsels:"

—Proverbs 1:5

"My son, attend unto my wisdom, and bow thine ear to my understanding; that thou mayest regard discretion, and that thy lips may keep knowledge."

2

Harsh Realities of Being a P.K.

There are some things that you need to realize to be able to succeed as a minister's child. Harsh realities that although seem to be unfair and irritating, they must be understood. I've compiled a list that was as exhaustive as I could make it. No doubt all of you could add one or two more that I missed. Now the harsh realities ...

1) Every thing you say and do will be watched, noticed, and critiqued.

The idea behind living in a glass house is that you have zero privacy. Your life is on public display to be enjoyed and manipulated by all who so desire. As a minister's child, people will watch you, I mean study you to see if you are real, to find cracks in the armor. They will watch how you handle problems to see if you are Christ-like. They will watch how you dress to see if you back up daddy's preaching. They will watch how you live from day to day, the main reason is to find any inconsistency in you, to give them an excuse to, first, have a host of inconsistencies in themselves and, second, to have a valid complaint toward the preacher. They want to believe that the apple never falls far from the tree. If you do something wrong, then your parents must do the same. This validates their reasoning to dismiss sin in their own life. Just know that always, you're being watched.

2) You are an example whether you like it or not.

"Let him that would move the world, first move himself."

—Socrates

Everything you do will be public interest. It will be talked about at the dinner tables of many of your church members. All of us are examples to someone! Some of us are used as examples of what to do and some of us as examples of what not to do. Which do you want to be? God gave us teaching on how to be a good example in His word. Let's look at it for a moment.

"Let no man despise thy youth but be thou an example of the believer, in word, in conversation, in charity, in spirit, in faith, in purity."

—I Timothy 4:12

Now notice, all of us are committed to be an example of the believer not just preacher's kids. Something we must remember over and over again, do what's right because it's right and it pleases God, not just because you're a pastor's kid! In other words, be good because you're a child of God, not because you're a child of a minister.

God tells us six areas of our lives that we should strive to be an example in.

(1) In word.

Your word should mean something. People should be able to rest secure in your word. It should be honorable, honest, and respected. One of the greatest compliments would be for people in the church to be able to say, "Well, if you said it, then it must be true!"

(2) In conversation.

What you talk about is important because it unveils what is in your heart to all who are listening. Hateful words or cursing is very damaging to your reputation as well as gossip, griping, whining, sarcasm, and dirty jokes. Let us remember that Peter learned this the hard way when he was accused of being a Christian. Three times he was accused of being a Christian and on the third time he cursed to prove he wasn't. Notice, there was no fourth accusation. A person's conversation can hurt his testimony quicker than anything else.

James was warning us of this reality when he wrote . . .

> *"For in many things we offend all. If any man offend not in word, the same is a perfect man, and able also to bridle the whole body. Behold , we put bits in the horses' mouths , that they may obey us; and we turn about their whole body. Behold also the ships, which though they be so great, and are driven of fierce winds, yet are they turned about with a very small helm, whithersoever the governor listeth. Even so the tongue is a little member, and boasteth great things. Behold, how great a matter a little fire kindleth! And the tongue is a fire, a world of iniquity: so is the tongue among our members, that it defileth the whole body, and setteth on fire the course of nature; and it is set on fire of hell. For every kind of beasts, and of birds, and of serpents, and of things in the sea, is tamed, and hath been tamed of mankind: But the tongue can no man tame; it is an unruly evil, full of deadly poison, Therewith bless we God, even the Father, and therewith curse we men, which are made after the similitude of God. Out of the same mouth proceedeth blessings and cursing. My brethren, these things ought not so to be."*
>
> — James 3:2-10

You must watch your conversation! Be careful what you talk about. Sometimes it's better to remain silent and retain your testimony than to join in and lose it.

(3) In Charity.

The word charity means love. To excel as a minister's kid you must be an example of love! Learn to love the work of God, the church, it's members, even your enemies. This is so hard to do! There will be times when people will hurt you and attack you and your first impulse will be to hate them but if you allow hate to manifest itself in you, it will lead to bitterness, spite, vengeance, depression, anxiety, unforgiveness, and clouded judgment. There are even health problems such as stress, heart disease, high blood pressure, ulcers, insomnia that result from hate. There are some people who are easy to love like the sweet widow lady or the nice old man who brings you gum every Sunday, but loving that deacon who is giving your dad the fifth degree or that woman who glares at your mother with hate boiling in her beady little eyes and that teenager who has everything and lets you know it every day; these people are much harder to show Christian love to. Jesus told us in the Word that if we love only those who are lovable; then we are no different from the heathen. It is and always has been the love of a Christian that sets us apart from the world. If God can love us in spite of all our sin and the countless times we let Him down and hurt Him, then surely we can find it in our heart to love others. By loving your church and it's members, you'll want to overlook their faults, reach out to them, and help them. If you'll show love and give love you'll get love!

"Cast your bread upon the water and thou shalt find it after many days."

—Ecclesiastes 11:1

"And now abideth faith, hope, charity, these three; but the greatest of these is charity."

—I Corinthians 13:13

(4) In Spirit.

A child of God and the child of a minister has got to have an enduring spirit. A spirit that is sweet and generous that SEEKS for good in all. If you can guard your spirit nothing can keep you down!

"The spirit of a man will sustain his infirmity: but a wounded spirit who can bear?"

—Proverbs 18:14

I always liked to believe that I could handle anybody and that no one could keep me from being happy. I felt that my spirit would keep me going when everything else said to quit. I'm simply trying to say that you can be an example of a good spirit to people who need to see a good spirit in a world full of bad spirit!

(5) In Faith.

As a minister's child it is important for you to develop faith!

Faith is possibly one of the hardest teachings of the Bible. I'll admit I don't like this thing about faith! I like to have everything in advance and I don't like having to depend on others or even God to supply. My human nature tells me that I can't trust anybody to take care of me, they'll only let me down. I must take care of myself! This is of course faulty reasoning and sinful (Romans 14:23). We must trust God and have a strong faith in Him! Faith has to be exercised and practiced as well as tested by God. You will need faith to survive all of the times when God will move your family, put your church in down spins, cause you to say goodbye to friends and family, to do the work of God. Let me caution you, a pastor and his family will have to live by faith. God will have it no other way. He will want you to know that He is in the driver seat and not you and He'll do things to constantly remind you to trust Him. Be careful about boasting in the strength of your faith because God will put it to the test, you will have trials and tribulations and God will know the truth about the depth of your faith.

> *"Knowing this, that the trying of your faith worketh patience."*
>
> —James 1:3

God will never let you have more than you can bear and with every trial He provides an escape.

"There hath no temptation taken you but such as is common to man; but God is faithful, who will not suffer you to be tempted above that ye are able; but will with the temptation also make a way to escape , that ye may be able to bear it."

—I Corinthians 10:13

Faith doesn't mean that there is no doubt or fear, it means choosing to believe in spite of doubt and fear! Don't lose your faith in God even if you lose it in men.

"The just shall live by faith"

—Galatians 3:11 b

"But without faith it is impossible to please him: for he that cometh to God must believe that he is, and that he is a rewarder of them that diligently seek him."

—Hebrews 11:6

Loss of faith is the reason most minister's kid are out of church. They perceive that God has in some way failed them and that instead of being their Saviour and friend, He is their enemy! What they have done is confused the let downs of people with the trials of God. Man is full of wickedness and selfishness, at best, they are still a disappointment. It is a must that you place your faith in God and God alone, not the deacons, other preachers, or folks in the church.

(6) In Purity.

There is so much that could be said here but I'll try to limit myself to just a few categories and trust your common sense to carry you the rest of the way. The Bible says so much about being pure. A child of God must dedicate himself to being pure. Now, we are all, at best, just sinners! (Romans 3:10, 23)

The Bible tells us in Isaiah . . .

"But we are all as an unclean thing, and all our righteousness are as filthy rags and we all do fade as a leaf;

and our iniquities, like the wind have taken us away."

—Isaiah 64:6

Notice, he says our righteousness; the best we have to offer. All of the good that is in us is like filthy rags. Filthy rags were the rags that the lepers used to cover the sores on their bodies. Outside of the town there would be a barrel or a fire pit and next to it strips of cloth were placed for the unfortunate people with leprosy. The old blood and puss infected strips were peeled away and burned. They were gross, full of wretched disease. Then, new rags would be applied to cover it up for a few days.

God says the best we have to offer are like those filthy rags that were burned in the fire! This is not a pretty picture. I'm saying this to point out the fact that we are just plain sinners who will make mistakes. A minister's kid shall not place the burden on themselves to be perfect because you will fail! However, you must strive to limit mistakes of sin as much as possible.

Paul wrote in Romans 12:1 - 2 . . .

"I beseech (beg)*you therefore, brethren by the mercies of God, that ye present your bodies a living sacrifice, holy, acceptable unto God, which is your reasonable service. And be not conformed to this world: but be ye transformed by the renewing of your mind, that ye may prove what is that good, and acceptable, and perfect, will of God."*

Romans 12: 1, 2

We are to present our bodies to God. Present means to dedicate, we are to dedicate our bodies to God for His service and righteousness. As a minister's kid there is a call to be an example in purity. You must be careful to date with rules and standards. You must watch the parties you go to and the friends you hang around. If you are with the wrong crowd you are the wrong crowd. Don't let peer pressure or the struggle to fit in and be one of the crowd make you try sinful acts such as alcohol, smoking or sex. You may think they like you because you're "down to earth" but they can never respect you again. You'll never be what you've got to be to be able to lead them out of it.

When a pastor's child falls into impurity it is very damaging to many other lives! Satan loves to entrap a P.K. because it leads him to many other quick victories. I knew a pastor who started a great church. He built it from the ground up and worked and scratched to make something of it. God blessed his work and it grew rapidly.

He had a fifteen year old daughter named Nancy* who had fallen for a young man who was not in church. Her parents begged her to not see this young man until he got into church. She rebelled and began to sneak out to see him. Nancy gave him her purity and at fifteen years old Nancy got pregnant! The news devastated her parents. Her dad went to the pulpit and resigned the next Sunday because he felt that he could not teach others how to raise a family and to be pure, when his own child didn't follow his preaching. Nancy told her boyfriend about the pregnancy but he being the mature, bright, loving young man that he was; told her that he wasn't responsible and that he wanted to break it off so he could date another girl. She was so shocked; she thought he loved her, meanwhile, her dad had to take a job selling cars to support the family. The once booming church was now in a downswing of disappointment and contention. Satan destroyed that church which later shut it's doors and the ministry of a once great preacher. All because of a P.K. who didn't take seriously the responsibility of being an example of purity. Nancy will stand before God accountable for a lot of people who she, by example, led astray. This is harsh but it's a reality of being a minister's child.

Purity must be regarded as important. There are many great books to teach you how to date as a Christian. Read

*Not her real name.

them and apply them, save yourself a lot of heartache and regret.

I'm trying to say that we have a responsibility to be examples to others. This can work for you if you'll let it. Once people trust you and respect you, you can reap benefits that are endless! But you can ruin a good testimony with one bad day or one season of sin.

"A good name is rather to be chosen than great riches, and loving favour rather than silver and gold."

—Proverbs 22:1

3) You won't be able to get away with what the other kids get away with.

This point used to drive me crazy! I could be with a group of kids doing something and I would be the only one that would get tagged for it! I'm sure you know this already but you need to understand that for you, what everybody else is doing won't be acceptable. They think that because you've been raised in a home where you've been taught better and had better examples that you should just naturally act better.

Now let me point out that God actually views it this way! Let me explain what I mean. Jesus told us in the book of Luke . . .

"But he that knew not and did commit things worthy of stripes, shall be beaten with few stripes. For unto whomsoever much is given, of him shall be much required: and to whom men have committed much, of him they will ask the more."

—Luke 12:48

By this verse alone we see the validation of such views. Jesus said to whom much is given, much is required. It is certainly fair to expect more from a Christian who has had the benefit of godly parents and a home dominated by the Word of God, over a child who has not had these things or has not had them to the degree or length of time that you've had them.

I believe God himself holds a minister's child to a higher level than others. Now don't get me wrong, what's right for one is right for all and what's wrong for one is wrong for all but God has given us P.K.'s privileges and with privilege comes responsibility and with kept responsibility comes reward. God rewards minister's kids who hold up to the added pressure. Let me explain it this way. When I was in high school I was elected captain of the basketball team. I was also one of the starting five.

My coach put a lot of pressure on me to be the spirit, energy, and leader of the team both on and off the court. It wasn't because he didn't like me or because he was out to get me, those responsibilities just came with the privilege to be the captain and a starter.

I also got many privileges to offset my burden of responsibility. Namely respect and authority two things that must be granted, they can't be stolen or bought. As a minister's kid people will expect more, but it's because they look up to you. Look at it as a compliment not as a criticism. The better you are, the more they expect! We are unique because we are elite! Just know that you are held to a higher standard than the other kids and walk cautiously because of it. Getting mad about it doesn't help and ignoring it only hurts you.

4) You will be left out of many events and avoided occasionally.

If you are what you are supposed to be then this will ring true often. The other kids will leave you out of a lot of parties, outings, nights on the town, trips to the mall, sleep-overs, trips, etc.

This happens for several reasons. First, they usually intend to do things that they know are not what a child of God should be doing, thus, they know you will have a problem with it and rain on their parade. Second, they're afraid that you'll report them and they'll be found out. Third, they know that your parents will be more suspicious and ask more questions about your activities. If you cave in and confess then they also know that a phone call from the pastor to their parents is imminent. Fourth, if you are with them and you are respected, you act as a visual conscious to them. If you are not there, then they can proceed with their naughty activities with less guilt. You will react to this as rejection or that there is something wrong with you that makes the others want to avoid you. However, the opposite is true. It's because there is something right with you that they can't attain, so to compensate for their incompetence they'll remove you from the equation.

Jesus said that a child of God must get used to rejection for his sake because he was rejected by men whose intentions were motivated by evil. You represent the light and the Bible says . . .

> *"And this is the condemnation, that light is come into the world, and men loved darkness rather than light, because their deeds were evil. For everyone that doeth evil hateth the light, neither cometh to the light, lest his deeds should be reproved."*
>
> —John 3:19-20

This verse sums it all up! It's not you that they reject it's the light and they don't want to see themselves for what they really are. I know it hurts and it will hurt you but try to remind yourself that it's not you, it's Jesus in you that they avoid. Jesus will reward you for every time you were rejected for his sake!

It helps to try to make up your own group and it also helps for you to be the primary organizer for the activities you attend so that you can have more control over what goes on. There are always people in your church who don't have many friends and they would love for you to call them and spend time with them. I've always liked having my own crowd more than being at the mercy of the "in crowd".

I've always had good, loyal, and godly friends this way. Be in control of the situation. You'll be surprised how many others need a friend and organizer.

5) You will be considered the enemy by the other kids.

I've already dealt with this but I want to add this, many times because your parents have to scold people, they may take it out on you and consider you an enemy. This is especially true if your dad has a Christian school. Expect others to be angry with you if your dad has to get on them. In their mind, you and your dad are one. It helps you to be loving and concerned for others when they get into trouble. Try to avoid making comments on it, even if asked.

Let them know that it was between them and the pastor and that you really don't know much about it and have nothing to do with it. A gentle hug or sweet note could let them know that you love them and that dad was just doing his job!

Another reason people will hate you is if you are called to make a stand for right. If this happens there's not much that can be done to avoid it. You have to be confident that you've done right and spoken the truth if they hate you for it, then, oh well.

> *"Am I therefore become your enemy, because I tell you the truth?"*
>
> —Galatians 4:16

> *"Let us have faith that right makes might, and in that faith, let us to the end, dare to do our duty, as we understand it."*
>
> —Abe Lincoln

6) You will hear information that you must not tell others.

There are things that you will hear in your home such as counseling sessions, confessionals, notes, discussions between your parents about church members, where privileged information is unveiled to you that would be very damaging if told to others.

It could be that you can hear your mom and dad in the other room discussing a big problem in the church. You didn't mean to hear and your parents didn't mean for you to hear it but there it is. Now what do you do?

Let me explain to you that your dad has what is called pastor-member confidentiality. This means that when he is told something in private it should stay in private. If you hear about Joe at church and how he has gotten into sin, then you go to school and tell your friends, then they tell others; it will probably get back to

Joe. Now there are several problems. Joe is humiliated and may leave church to save face. He's also angry at the fact that the only person he trusted to tell this to was his pastor. Now he blames the man of God for telling what was supposed to be private. The result is this, your dad will lose his credibility as a private counselor and he will not be able to properly help his flock. He will also get tagged a gossip which will cause many to disrespect him. You must keep the things you hear in home; at home! The juicy information you are blabbing could ruin someone's life and chances for restitution and substantially hurt dad's credibility as a confidential counselor.

> "He that is void of wisdom despiseth his neighbor: but a man of understanding holdeth his peace. A tale bearer revealeth secrets: but he that is of a faithful spirit concealeth the matter."
>
> —Proverbs 11:12, 13

The Bible says that a wise person doesn't tell all that he knows. Remember the golden rule? If you wouldn't want your intimate secrets told abroad then you shouldn't do it to others. Keep your mouth shut and your conscious clear.

> *"I will speak ill of no man, and speak all the good I know of everybody."*
>
> —Benjamin Franklin

7) You will see the human side of a man of God. "Familiarity breeds contempt."

The one, who all others refer to as "Pastor", is that same one you call dad. I always called my dad, dad, because there is no greater way to bestow respect on him than to refer to him as dad. Many men can be my pastor but only one man can be my dad. Now, I was very close to my dad and did a lot of things with him. I got to see him at his best and worst. Those days when he was close to God and walking on air and those days when he was in the depths of despair. You must realize something: now listen to me so I can save you much bitterness down the road! Now, your dad has been called of God to preach the Gospel. He is, however, just a man, made of flesh and blood. He's imperfect and still has a sinful heart that he fights daily, just as you do! He will make mistakes, lots of them!

Mistakes in fatherhood, in pastoring, as a husband, and as a sinner saved by grace. It's unfair for you to throw the burden of perfection on him when God says that no one can bear that. You don't want people to expect flawless living from you, your dad doesn't want it either. You will see the best and the worst of the man of God you call dad. You need to cut him some slack and not view him as a hypocrite or fake. Realize he's doing the best he can. God deals with his men and doesn't need your help to punish them. The walls of glass are fragile enough as it is. Your dad shouldn't have to worry about his most painful attacks coming from his own flesh and blood.

Once I was talking to the son of a certain pastor. After a few moments of conversation I could see that this boy didn't respect his dad. He said, "Everybody thinks my dad is so perfect but I could tell them different!" He went on to call his dad a phony and a hypocrite. Now, I'm sure he knew his dad much better than I did, but my only opinion of this boy was that he was a punk! If your dad isn't at home the way he is at church then pray for him and be good in spite of it. God uses those who are willing to serve not just those who are perfect. Which I must say I'm glad because that means that God can use a sinner like me and one like you. God used Moses, David, and Paul, three men who were murderers. God used Noah, the first alcoholic of the Bible. God used Peter, a man who denied God and quit the ministry! If God can use those men with such huge faults, then He can use your dad with his faults.

"He that is without sin among you, let him first cast a stone at her."

—John 8:7

8) You will receive more responsibilities at church.

Your mom and dad will often call upon you to do such tasks as mowing the church lawn, cleaning the church, filling the baptistry, taking out the trash, setting up the Sunday school rooms or fellowship hall, pick people up for church, sing, teach, work bus routes, go soul winning, and various other jobs that are undesirable.

This leads a lot of P.K.'s to feelings of being taken advantage of, exploited, and just feeling like the church slave. I know it's a pain to do jobs that no one else will do because your dad knows you won't leave the church over it and it's not fair but as long as there are P.K.'s the injustice will continue. Just remember that if you do it with the right attitude, then God sees it and will reward you accordingly. If you complain about it, then, you lose God's reward. What a shame it would be to do all that work and lose the reward! Just do it for Jesus and serve with gladness of heart.

9) You will most likely move several times throughout your childhood.

This is a hard reality of being a minister's kid. If your dad's an evangelist then you'll live on the road. Lots of evangelist's kids are home schooled and travel most of the year. Lots of them find it hard to meet deep friends and dating has a special challenge added to it. It is hard to develop relationships without time to develop them!

A pastor's kid will most likely move several times as their dad will go from church to church. Statistics show us that the average pastor will stay about two to three years at a church. This means that if you live at home for eighteen years then you will move about six times. Moving is a mixed bag of emotions. On one hand you are excited about a new town, new school, new church, new vision, new house, and new friends. But on the other hand it's hard to say goodbye, pack boxes, move furniture, break in new friends, and be willing to get attached to things because you know you'll just have to endure the pain of leaving it behind. My family moved several times while I was at home and I've moved four times since I've been on my own. More than once I've felt the butterflies of a nervous stomach as I went to a new school, (I went to three high schools in four years!), a new church or the first night in a new room. I've seen my mom unpack the shattered remains of valuable family heirlooms. It's a hard part of the ministry. All I can say is that you can survive it. You have to try to look on the bright side and make the most of it. A strong family can survive frequent moves. Those moves made my brothers and I the best of friends as there were times when we were the only teenagers we knew. Those are some of my sweetest memories now as an adult. This is just something that we must suffer for Jesus and trust God. If your dad pastors one church for all of your childhood, then, praise God, you're lucky! Most of us won't have that testimony.

10) You will see and hear bad examples of Christianity.

Remember, as a church worker, you are a nurse in the hospital for the spiritually sick. Don't let Christians who are hypocrites and ungodly rob you of the joy of serving God. These people will stand before God accountable! Don't let a few bad examples disenchant you with the thousands of real, honest Christians. You will see the ugliness of people and some of them will be deacons, staff members, teachers, and people who claimed to be a friend of your family.

My papaw (who pastored over forty years) told me the one who meets you at the door and greets you will most likely be the one who sticks the knife in your back first. After years of church work I must say he was so right. I've seen men who act like such good Christians turn into hateful, spiteful, horrible people. I've seen business meetings turn into riots. I've also lived long enough to see how God dealt with them. No one comes out ahead by doing opposite of God's will. Keep your eye on God and not on men and you'll never get discouraged. The problem is in people not the church or God's work.

11) You will see your family attacked.

"He who reigns within himself and rules his passions, desires, and fears is more than a king."

—Milton

This is a hard one. This is one reality that I was never able to get used to. As I've already stated, the church is full of people who do dumb things. I've seen my dad attacked by people in the church more than I wish. Most P.K.'s will endure this especially if your dad is a hell-fire, old fashioned preacher as mine is. I remember every time someone would attack us I would want to counterattack and defend the honor of my family. My dad would restrain all such ideas. I would get so mad and sometimes I felt like a spineless wimp! Dad said God will take care of us just keep serving Him and doing what's right, they'll lose if we stay right. I didn't understand it then but now I do.

There are some things that you must realize on this subject. When you or your family are attacked you are in such an unfair position because you can't defend yourself. The more you fight the more people will turn on you. People perceive you as the stronger one and they'll pull for the underdog, even if they are wrong. If you defend yourself you will give more attention to your attackers which gives them a stronger voice. When you ignore them they become disarmed. "A soft answer turneth away wrath." I always thought about how God protected Moses from all of his attackers. It seemed like every time he turned around there was an uprising against him. It seemed that no matter what God did for them or how much Moses proved his leadership and love, someone had it out for him. God opened the ground and swallowed up one group and sent snakes to bite and kill another group. Every time Moses was challenged God fought for him. There are other examples in the Bible of God's protection. I think we know what the Bible says about God's protection, the question is, do we have faith in it. All I can say is, God is able to protect us. The key is, stay next to His side, do what He says, do right and watch God in action.

I've lived long enough to read several formal letters of apology from people who have attacked my family. I've read where God dealt with them and humbled them. Cancer, disease, bankruptcy, death, and all sorts of tribulations have knocked on the door of those who have dared to raise their sword against God's anointed.

"But they that wait upon the Lord shall renew their strength; they shall mount up with wings as eagles; they shall run, and not be weary; and they shall walk, and not faint."

—Isaiah 40:31

"For in the time of trouble he shall hide me in his pavilion: in the secret of his tabernacle shall he hide me; he shall set me upon a rock."
—Psalm 27:5

"But the Lord is my defense; and my God is the rock of my refuge."

—Psalm 94:22

It is not if your family is attacked, it is when your family is attacked. Make sure that you keep silent, keep in prayer, ignore their criticism, speak only to deep trusted friends (be careful, anything you say to them, they can say to others), don't get on the offensive and let God do what he's promised to do. In the end you'll still be standing. Dr. Bob Jones Sr. once said, "Do right, do right, until the stars fall down; do right."

"By taking revenge, a man is but even with his enemy; but in passing over it, he is superior."

—Baron

"We cannot control the evil tongues of others; but a good life enables us to disregard them."

—Cato

12) You will be used as the excuse when you get into trouble with others.

Just get ready to hear those famous words "The pastor's kid did it." It's coming! The others know that they can blame their actions on bad leadership and some how get away with it. This, of course, just makes you look worse in the eyes of everyone.This is another reason to be careful and keep out of trouble!

13) There will be times when you must take a backseat to other's priorities and schedules.

You know what I'm saying. It's your birthday and dad has promised to take you out for the day. You get to pick out any new outfit. You're so excited and you've waited a whole year for this date to come. You and dad are just about to head to the car when the phone rings. It's a crying, frantic voice on the other end. "Preacher, we need you, it's an emergency." Maybe it's someone in the hospital or someone's died, maybe their husband has left them and they need immediate attention. All you know is this, dad is saying, "Son, I'll make it up to you", as he's rushing off. I don't care what the cause is, it hurts and it's disappointing.

These days will happen, it's a reality of being a P.K. Just expect them. Now, this doesn't just happen to P.K.'s. Businessmen, doctors, soldiers, lawyers, factory workers; they all have unexpected emergencies that call them away. It could be worse! Dad could be going to war or to fight a fire, or to arrest a dangerous criminal, or he could just be going to make another buck. At least you know that dad is usually doing something worthwhile.

You have to remind yourself that, first, dad is just as disappointed as you are and was planning to spend his valuable time with you and circumstances aren't always under his control. Second, God will bless you for giving up your valuable time for his sake. Sometimes dad will be gone preaching revivals and funerals, or doing "preacher" things. Every job has it's drawbacks. Time consumption is a problem in the ministry. Every one wants a piece of dad's time. If you feel neglected, ask your parents to sit down and talk. Tell them your needs and concerns.

Let them know that you miss personal time and desire it. Ask your parents for a day in advance to spend with you. Most parents think that it's not that important to you. You must assure them that it is.

14) There will be snobs that will try to make you feel unimportant.

Let me demonstrate this point by sharing this story. When I was about thirteen years old, a wealthy family in the church had a son who is about two years older than me. He had a whole closet full of suits and polo shirts, designer clothes worth a small fortune. Once a year they would have a big yard sale when they would sell their son's clothes. I come from a family with five kids in it. Mom did a great job keeping clothes on us but sometimes we had to catch the bargains. At thirteen I was starting to notice styles and felt the pressure to dress with the "in" crowd. My parents couldn't afford name brands but once a year this yard sale was my big chance to have a shirt with a name brand on it. The family always gave us a chance to come early to the yard sale and get first pick, (which I really do appreciate and feel grateful for.)

When I got to the yard sale I noticed this awesome gray polo suit. It was a $500 dollar suit that had been worn twice. Mom bought it for me and I was so proud of it. I could hardly wait to wear it the next Sunday. I walked into Sunday school and some of my friends said, "Hey, look at Riggs, the sharp dressed man". I was the fashion statement, the man of the hour when suddenly rain fell on my parade! The son of this wealthy family said, "That used to be mine, you've been to our yard sale, haven't you?" I was so embarrassed. Maybe I shouldn't have let it bother me, but it did. I did try to maintain dignity. There was always a group of kids who tried to make me feel beneath them. Rich kids, popular kids, deacon's kids, they seemed to have a better than thou attitude. At times I'd find myself like a dog under the table trying to gather the scraps they'd throw me. I guess every child has to deal with this in some sort or another. All I can say is, that success is the best revenge. Years from now, none of this will matter. A lot of the kids couldn't survive without daddy's money to keep them going. Never let them make you think they are better than you. You'd be surprised if you knew how many of them think you've got it all and that you're probably spoiled or stuck up.

15) You will be used as an example to the other kids which will cause them to resent you.

"Why can't you be more like the pastor's kid," is a phrase that many of your peers will hear when they are in trouble. Comparisons to you will lead the other kids to resent you and to look for inconsistencies in your life to even the score. This is one of the burdens of being an example. If you are good and you try to do what's right then this is going to be inevitable. The other parents will use you to try to motivate their child to do better or to follow your lead. This can, of course, come at your expense. Do your best to not be a condescending spirit around the other kids. You can be loving and supportive as well as friendly to them at church and school without hanging around them or joining them in evil. If the other kids respect you and know that you've got a right spirit then they will not take this out on you as much.

16) You will hear stories of your life used as illustrations by your dad in church sermons.

I can remember it so well, the church was full, I was on the second row in the youth section trying to act cool and wanting all the others to perceive me as a man whose got it all together. It would all be going so well when my dad would be up there preaching away when suddenly he would tell how a few weeks ago Rusty had done something and how he had to spank me and how I got in trouble. I remember hearing the other kids snicker, I could feel them leering at me. I could feel my face turning red. All I could do was smile and say "Amen". I would also hear many private family events spoken publicly in the pulpit. Now, my dad did this early in his ministry. My mother came to her babies rescue on this by talking to dad and pointing out that we were not little children anymore and that this was embarrassing to us and that it hurt our dignity. Dad asked us if it bothered us for him to use us as illustrations. We had to say that honestly, it did. If he told good things then we looked like kiss ups to our friends, if he told bad things then we had our friends kidding us about it. We felt like we lost either way.

If your dad does this and it bothers you, maybe you could get your mother to speak to him or go to him yourself and tell him, now that you are older you wish to keep your private life, private. I'm sure that he'll probably be defensive at first but he'll think about it and then he'll see it your way. I'm sure that your dad is probably like mine. He just didn't realize that it bothered you or hurts you. A good understanding makes for a long friendship.

17) You will have many people in the church who think they are your parents.

It seems that sometimes churches look at a pastor and his family as property of the church. They think that they have the right to pry into your business sometimes. As I was growing up there were people who seemed to watch me like I was one of their kids. They would scold me, lecture me, and even in some rare cases spank me (school teachers). This will be a problem for some P.K.'s. It will be especially bad if your dad has staff members. Most of them were great. I got along quite well with them. They did their job and let my parents do their job.

There were, however, those who felt that it was up to them to raise me. They would lecture me for hours and they seemed to watch me like a hawk. I'm sure that their intentions were noble but it's affect was adverse. At the time I felt picked on or somehow singled out. There were feelings of anger and resentment at times toward them. I wanted to tell them that I had two perfectly good parents and that I didn't need another parent! Now, I realize that they were good people and meant well, they were trying to help me in their own way.

This problem can be worse in some situations. For instance if you go to the Christian school at your church, this is going to be something that will happen to you. Remind yourself that they are just trying to help. The people who will do it the most are deacons, youth pastors, assistant pastors, Sunday school teachers, school teachers, friends of your parents, etc.

You may wish to talk to your parents and have them speak to the ones who seem to do this. Your parents can tell them that although they appreciate their help; they do have a plan concerning raising you and that "parenting" needs to be left to us, your parents. In most cases, you can handle it by being polite and just letting them talk. Take the good advise and ignore the rest. You can eat fish and pick out the bones. Try to read the intention behind the words. Sometimes, they intend to hurt, belittle, or even provoke you to wrath but most of the time love is the motive. It is possible to be right in your position, but wrong in your disposition. Many folks know what they want to say they just don't do a good job relaying their message to you and it comes out offensive or belittling to you. Look at who is saying it more than what's being said.

I know of a P.K. who preached for his dad while his dad was out of town. After the sermon the young P.K. went to the door to shake hands and greet people on their way out of the church. As he was there, one of the men came up to him and critiqued his message. This hurt his feelings and it left him feeling insecure about his preaching ability. The man is a good, dear friend of his family and truly loves him. He had zero intentions to hurt him. He just felt his "fatherly" advise would be welcomed. His dad spoke to the man about the incident and when he realized that his advise was taken wrongly he was deeply sorry. He cried and said, "I wouldn't hurt one of your kids for anything. I thought I was helping". He and the young P.K. had worked it out and are still friends. I believe this happens more often than not. Good intentions, just bad judgment.

18) Your actions can cause your dad to be fired.

I don't believe there's too many men who could actually lose their job and be destroyed by not just their own actions and sins but for those of their family. Let's face it, a manager of Walmart won't be fired if his child gets caught smoking dope or gets pregnant. I know of many good pastors who've stayed out of trouble, lived right, avoided temptations, but have been asked to resign because of their kids. I think that this is one unique aspect of being a P.K. You see the Bible teaches a very important requirement for preachers. They must rule well their own family.

"One that ruleth well his own house, having his children in subjection with all gravity; (For if a man know not how to rule his own house, how shall he take care of the church of God?)

—I Timothy 3:4, 5

In the word of God it is imperative that a preacher be able to control his family. The feeling is this, if a preacher can't handle his own kids and if his own kids and wife don't even respect him or his teachings then how can you expect people in the church to listen and to respect what he teaches? In most cases, this verse will condemn your dad to failure if you go into sin. He will feel like a hypocrite to teach on parenting or on how to have a godly home. He will not be able to counsel people as effectively when they are having problems with their kids.

The bottom line is this, as a minister's child what you do affects so much more than just you. Your dad can reap what you sow. It doesn't matter if we like it or not, we just don't have the luxury of making huge sinful mistakes. P.K.'s who run away, do drugs, rebel, quit church, get pregnant, drink, smoke, and basically don't live righteous are hurting your mom and dad more than they can ever know. Not only does it hurt them the way it hurts all parents but it also hurts them from a career standpoint also.

I know several men who used to be pastors and now are out of the ministry selling cars or insurance and it's no fault of their own. It's because of their kids living in sin. One of two things will happen if you sow your wild oats concerning your dad. One: The church will fire him and use I Timothy 3: 4, 5 as their biblical grounds (and be just in their actions). Two: our dad will keep his job but he'll just be a figurehead for no one will respect his leadership or his teachings.

You can do whatever you want. Just remember this, you will answer to God. God protects his preachers. God will protect your dad from onslaughts, attacks, demonic influence, and even you.

"Touch not mine anointed, and do my prophets no harm."

—Psalm 105:15

I'll never forget about Freddy*, Freddy was about twenty years old and a P.K. His dad pastored a church that ran about 150 people. My dad was preaching a revival in Freddy's church . Freddy's dad asked my dad to try to talk to Freddy. He said that Freddy had become very rebellious and that he was set on doing wrong. Dad said, "Sure I'll talk to him."

So he went over to see Freddy before church that night. Dad put his hand on his shoulder and asked him what was bothering him. Freddy just shrugged dad's hand off his shoulder and angrily stared at the T.V. As dad tried to talk, Freddy just got up and walked into his room and shut the door. That night dad was shocked, Freddy had shown up for church. He walked in and sat on the front row. Dad got up to preach on a subject that every preacher has a sermon on; "Be sure your sins will find you out."

About half way through dad's sermon Freddy jumped up as if something was said that made him mad! He rudely stomped down the aisle and he slammed the door as hard as he could in the face of that country preacher. (No he didn't, he slammed that door in the face of God Almighty!) The next day, dad and Freddy's dad were out on visitation when a car pulled up behind them with lights blinking on and off and the horn blasting. The preacher said, "That's my daughter, what in the world." He then pulled over. His daughter ran up to the window with breathless, frantic words and a distorted, tear stained face screaming, "Freddy, Freddy, oh my God, it's Freddy". After she calmed down enough she explained that there was an accident at Freddy's work and that twenty year old Freddy was crushed to death! Freddy was dead. Dad said that he felt so helpless as he watched Freddy's dad grab the steering wheel with both hands and beat his head against it lamenting and crying, "No, no, God, I told him you were going to get him, no, no, God, no!"

Even as a P.K. you must respect and honor the man of God. You must walk right and strive to be righteous. None of us enjoy this reality but it's just the way it is and the way it will always be.

I can understand it if your parents are horrible people who live one way at church and another way at home. If they beat you

*not his real name.

or abuse you or if they are into sin themselves. This is not the case most of the time. In most of the P.K.'s I've known who have gone bad it was simply the P.K. who rebelled against their parents and against God. If you are rebellious you will cost your mom, your dad, your church and most importantly yourself far more than you're willing to pay.

> "*Be not deceived: God is not mocked: for whatsoever a man soweth that shall he also reap.*" - Galatians 6:7

> "*For every one that curseth his father or his mother shall be surely put to death: he hath cursed his father or mother; his blood shall be upon him.*"
>
> —Leviticus 20:9

> "*But if ye will not do so, behold, ye have sinned against the Lord: and be sure your sin will find you out.*"
>
> —Numbers 32:23

> "*Sin will take you farther than you want to go, keep you longer than you want to stay, cost you more than you want to pay.*"
>
> —author unknown

19) You can do hundreds of ignored good things and be remembered for one bad thing.

> "*It is better to be nobly remembered than to be nobly born.*"
>
> —Ruskin

Trouble makes news! When was the last time a man was on the news for not robbing a bank? Tragedy or shocking news is what makes the headlines. This just backs up the other reasons for you to stay out of trouble at all costs. What you wish to be remembered for later you must be now!

> "*And there's a lust in man no charm can tame of loudly publishing our neighbor's shame on eagle's wings immortal scandals fly while virtuous actions are but born and die.*"
>
> —Stephen Harvey

20) You will feel pressure to enter the ministry.

I remember as a little boy people saying to me, "Are you going to be a preacher like your dad some day?" And when I did surrender to preach, people said, "So, you're following in your dad's footprints?" Now, I did enter the ministry but not because my dad is in the ministry. I did it for the only reason that's biblical, because I felt sure that God wanted me and created me to be a preacher of the Gospel. To be a minister is one of the greatest, if not the greatest of callings that can be bestowed upon one. Yet it is a calling, a decision of God. There are, unfortunately, many young people who enter the ministry whether it be surrendering to be a preacher's wife, becoming a school teacher, or a youth director, or even going into the music ministry who are NOT called of God. They do it because they feel that mom and dad want it or that the church expects it. A lot of times this pressure is purely self inflicted. In reality, no one is making you do anything, you just think that they won't like you, or think that you are out of God's will unless you go into some type of ministry. You need to do what God wants first and above all. God may want you to be a medical doctor or a lawyer or a Christian businessman who sends thousands of dollars into the ministry. God may even want you to be a factory worker or a plumber. If God wants you to do something for Him, He'll first convict you of it through the Holy Spirit's leading. You'll just know that this is what God made you for. It will just fit. Second, God will empower you to do what He's called you to do. In other words, He'll give you the gifts and talents to do what He's calling you to do. God will never ask you to do something that's impossible. For instance, I'm not a singer! When I sing, heavens flag flies at half mast and the angels begin to weep! My singing talents would not be a blessing to anyone. By this, I know that God never intended for me to be a minister of music. God gave me talents that I use every day as a pastor. God never asks you to do a job without also giving you the gifts to accomplish it. Third, God will lead you by opening and shutting doors to reveal His will to you. God will just bring opportunities your way or shut the door on other opportunities. Sometimes God just takes charge of the situation and makes you do what He wants. For more information on this subject read the book of Jonah in the Bible. God has a will for you, a purpose for your life. You must diligently search for it as a young person and do it for there and only there lies peace for you. You must pray for direction and discernment to know God's plan. Remember the devil has a will for you too and if you follow him it will lead to destruction in your life. If you enter the ministry for the wrong reason, you are out of God's will and you won't be happy serving God. Bitterness and resentment will well up inside you. You will find it tempting to quit during the hard times and turmoil of the ministry. You must be sure that you are called of God and not of man. I know some P.K.'s who are wonderful Christians but are not in full time Christian service. They do go soul winning, attend church regularly, teach Sunday schools and are bus workers. They are great Christians who serve God, they just don't do it for a living. There is nothing wrong with this if it's God's will. My parents never encouraged me to be a preacher, they just wanted me to be a good Christian and please God with my life. You will find what God wants if you are searching for it! Whatever talent God has given you, find a way to use it for Him in some way. Read I Corinthians 12 for some great insight on this subject.

> *". . . stir up the gift of God, which is in thee. . ."*
>
> —II Timothy 1:6

> *"And God hath set some in the church, first apostles, secondarily prophets, thirdly teachers, after that miracles then gifts of healing, helps, governments, diversities of tongues."*
>
> —I Corinthians 12:28

> *"Now there are diversities of gifts, but the same spirit. And there are differences of administrations, but the same Lord. And there are diversities of operations, but it is the same God which worketh all in all. But the manifestation of the spirit is given to every man to profit withal."*
>
> —I Corinthians 12:4-7

21) You will be expected to have biblical knowledge as a young person that takes years to possess.

"You should know this because your dad is the preacher". How many times have you heard that one? I've had people drill me in the Bible and act shocked when I didn't understand it all. It takes years to gain a working knowledge of the Bible! The more I study it the more I see how incredible, how deep and rich it is! The more I understand the Bible, the more I see how little I understand God's word. No one is a complete authority on the word of God!

It's unfair for you or anybody else to expect you to know what took your dad years of Bible college, Sunday school, personal study, reading, and being taught. You should be advanced because of your atmosphere and environment. For instance if your dad is a plumber, then, you will probably know more about plumbing than the kid whose dad runs a pet shop. As a P.K. you will know a lot about the Bible because you are exposed to it often. You still must study on your own and have a hunger for knowledge and wisdom.

Don't let it rattle you if someone asks you a Bible question and you don't know the answer. It happens to us all. Tell them, "Let me look into that and think about it and I"ll get back with you." There's no shame in not knowing only in not caring!

"Yea, if thou cries after knowledge, and liftest up thy voice for understanding; if thou seekest her as silver, and searches for her as for hid treasures; then shalt thou understand the fear of the Lord, and find the knowledge of God."

—Proverbs 2:3-5

"I love them that love me; (wisdom) and those that seek me early shall find me".

—Proverbs 8:17

"Study to shew thyself approved unto God, a workman that needeth not to be ashamed, rightly dividing the word of truth."

—II Timothy 2:15

"Study rather to fill your mind than your coffers; knowing that gold and silver were originally mingled with dirt, until avarice or ambition parted them!"

—Seneca

"Whoso neglects learning in his youth, loses the past and is dead for the future."

—Euripides

22) You will be targeted by the devil.

A P.K. must be aware that the devil is out to get you more than any other child. He will go after you because getting you gives him a greater prize. I believe that the demonic attacks on P.K.'s are great and that the devil concentrates much of his forces to bring down the children of ministers.

I read one time that witches will cast spells intended to bring down men of God and that they will target his family. They will conjure up dark forces of demonic oppression to attack and destroy preacher's kids.

A P.K. who is out of church is like a soldier is an open field. He is easy prey for the snipers that Satan has employed. It is my belief that all P.K.'s need to be more careful because the devil wants us more!

3
Helpful Hints

In the next few pages I'm going to give you some "Tricks of the Trade". I want to give you some ideas that will help you be a better minister's kid and to help you excel as a P.K. I hope these ideas will help you to find a groove in the church and also to help you maintain the proper perspective of being a P.K. These ideas are proven to work and they will make you more aware of how you can be a help to your dad, your church, your friends, and most importantly to God.

1) Look at the church as your church and not just dad's church.

I hear a lot of P.K.'s refer to their church as dad's church. I don't like that train of thought! It's your church too and you need to develop a love, respect, and pride for it. A better way to refer to the church is "our" church. P.K.'s who see the church as nothing more than their dad's workplace usually don't have a proper love for the church. A personal love from inside them. They also seem to not care about it's well being or how it's doing, that's dad's problem. It's also your problem because it affects your life. If dad gets discouraged and feels alone at church, then you most likely will be loading up a U-Haul and heading to another church in another town far away with a new house and new friends and new schools! If you like where you live then your best bet is to help, encourage, and pray for your church as much as possible. Deep love for the church from the entire family will ground you there. It's also what will help build that church. Love is what everybody needs and wants. Make the church your church and put a little bit of yourself forever embedded into it. You'll be surprised how this will help you develop a love for the church. Jesus describes the church as his bride. You must fall in love with the church personally.

2) Get involved with the work of the church.

"Light is the task where many share the toil."

—Homer

There are so many opportunities for God's service available to a minister's kid in the church. I believe that it's essential for you to be involved with the church work to be able to fall in love with it. If you work to build something you have so much more pride in it as well as a protection for it. If I were to walk into the high school of your town and look at the trophies in the trophy case, I wouldn't feel one ounce of pride or sentiment for it. No memories of glory and pain or victory would fill my mind. Why? Because I didn't go to school there, I wasn't on their team rosters. I didn't help in any way to achieve that honor. Therefore, I can not share in the glory or pride. Now if you go to the trophy case of Hot Springs Christian Academy where I played for the 1985 state champions or to Koolau Baptist Academy in Hawaii where I played for the 1987 state championships or to Redemption Academy where I was on the 1988 state championship team you'll see a marked difference in my response. I will well up with pride as I remember how hard we worked and all the teams we had to beat to get that award. Why? Because I was involved with the work that went into the success, therefore I was able to share in the pride, glory, and the great memories involved.

In my church, I look at it the same. I want to be able to rejoice when my church is rejoicing, feel pride when my church is bragged on, feel anger when my church is criticized, be able to say thank you when my church is complimented. The only way this can be possible is for me to be involved in the work that either makes or breaks my church.

There is nothing like the feeling when a family you invited joins the church or when a person you invited gets saved and baptized, to see a child off your bus route get saved or surrender to preach. When I look at the church my dad pastored, I can be proud of it because I know I helped build it in my own way. Get involved with the soul winning, bus routes, usher program, Sunday school program and help it be a success.

A lot of preacher's kids don't get involved in the work because they don't feel that they have anything to offer or are too young to help. You'd be surprised what you can do even at a young age. God has used young people all through history. David was just a teenager when he engaged and defeated Goliath in battle. Daniel was a boy when he was taken captive by Babylon and made an immediate impact. Shadrach, Meshach, and Abednego were young when they refused to bow to Nebuchadnezzar's image. In more modern history, Alfred Tennyson wrote his first volume at eighteen years old. Beethoven wrote some of his greatest works as a child.

I was fifteen years old when I became a bus captain and I was only eighteen when I started Starlight Youth Ministries, nineteen when I went full time as a youth pastor, twenty-four when I started the All-Star Youth Conference and the Soldiers of the Cross Christian Youth Camp. At twenty-five I became a pastor. The only reason I was young when God allowed me to step up to service is because I started young.

Ask your dad if you can have an area of responsibility. It may be taking out all the trash and sweeping the floors. It may be filling the baptistry, mowing the grass, changing the marquee on the church sign, or placing water on the pulpit for the speakers. As you get older or if you are a mature P.K. you may be able to handle such jobs as teaching a Sunday school class, being a bus captain, driving the church bus or van, directing the music, working with the youth, singing in choir, working in the children's church, helping in the office, or being in charge of a department. I remember my first job at the church, I was a gopher on the bus route. My dad tried to help us find ways to work for God at church very early. My sister Christy was twelve when dad put her in charge of the tape ministry. She would copy the tapes and label them. Having a small job at church gave me a love and pride for my church and it made me feel important and needed. It also created a desire to be used of God in bigger areas as I grew and matured.

> *"He also that is slothful in his work is brother to him that is a great waster."*
>
> —Proverbs 18:9

> *"He becometh poor that dealeth with a slack hand: but the hand of the diligent maketh rich. He that gathereth in summer is a wise son: but he that sleepeth in harvest is a son that causeth shame."*
>
> —Proverbs 10:4 & 5

3) Dress up for church.

I believe that you should wear the best clothes you have to church. I don't believe that God intended for us to dress for church the same way we dress when we go to the mall! We are at church to worship the King of Kings and Lord of Lords. I think we should dress with respect. Jeans and a t-shirt are great for playing out in the yard but not for worshiping God Almighty. It's not that it's a sin to wear those things to church. It's just not the way an ambassador should dress. The Bible says . . .

> *"Now then we are ambassadors for Christ, as though God did beseech you by us; we pray you in Christ's stead, be ye reconciled to God."*
>
> —II Corinthians 5:20
>
> *"A wicked messenger falleth into mischief: but a faithful ambassador is health."*
>
> —Proverbs 13:17

Can you imagine if the evening news showed a U.S. ambassador at a big event representing the United States in a t- shirt and jeans or a wrinkled shirt with dirty pants? No, then how much more should we dress for success in representing the Lord and the church. At least on Sunday morning try to dress up.

People will treat you different when you are dressed sharp. One time I went to the mall with a friend. We went to an expensive department store wearing jeans and polo type shirts. We were neat and clean just dressed down. We noticed that it seemed hard to get a sales representative to assist us. A few weeks later I went back to that store, it was on a Sunday and I was in a suit and tie. Within ten seconds of entering the store I had a sales representative attached to me and trying really hard to make me happy! How you dress makes a difference in the way people perceive you and treat you. If you want respect, then dressing for it is helpful. Business clothes are designed for respect and I must admit, not for comfort but there is a time to dress up and a time to dress down. Church is a dress up time. Just try dressing up for a while and see if people at church don't treat you a little different.

4) Sit up front during service.

I don't understand preachers kids that sit in the back during church. When I was a youth pastor I hated to see teens and kids on the back row. I hated it so much that I had a youth section reserved on the first four rows on the right side of the auditorium. I noticed that the kids who refused to sit there always sat on the back row and always for the same reason, to cut up, pass notes, come in and out, sleep, talk, and be a distraction to all around them. I used to wonder why those kids even came to church! I've never seen good, godly, respectable kids sit on the back row. If I'm at a church and the pastor's kids sit on the back rows, it is a huge indication of their backslidden and rebellious spiritual condition. You may say that you are the exception but people judge by what is the norm and not the exception. If you are in the back row, you will be perceived as rebellious.

I can't tell you how many times I was complimented on the fact that I always sat up front. People notice it. The other kids also will sit up front more if you'll do it. This is a simple but very effective tip to help you be the kind of P.K. that is respected and trusted instead of one that is typical of the P.K.'s who have given all of us a bad name.

5) Attend all church functions.

A great way to build rapport with the church is by attending all the functions possible. I'm talking about going to weddings, funerals, revivals, school events, church parties, activities, baby and wedding showers, etc. I've been to funerals where there was just two or three people there and weddings where most of the people didn't show. It meant a lot to them that their pastor's son cared enough to come. You will receive a very special blessing when you attend such functions. People will view you as a thoughtful, compassionate, and caring individual. Who knows, you may be the inspiration behind them better attending church functions themselves. I always enjoyed those functions or at least I enjoyed knowing I was a blessing to another just by being there. We can't always help the way we wish we could help, but we can just be there sometimes. That shoulder to cry on or that life of the party, that one friend who is guaranteed to be supportive. Most people only attend what interests them. A true friend is interested in what interests his friends. The greatest gift one can give is time. Time can never be redeemed. Whoever it's spent on is the possessor of it for eternity. If you are a giving person then this will make sense to you. If you are selfish then this tip will seem foolish.

> *"There was a man, though some did count him mad, the more he cast away, the more he had."*
>
> —John Bunyan

> *"Give, and it shall be given unto you; good measure, pressed down, and shaken together and running over, shall men give into your bosom. For with the same measure that ye mete withal it shall be measured to you again."*
>
> —Luke 6:38

6) As often as possible, give a testimony.

A church testimony service is a great time for a minister's kid to make a great impression! Take advantage of this opportunity to get to say a few words. I believe that it's good to give a testimony for several reasons. Let me share them with you.

(A) It's encouraging to others.

(B) It encourages others to share what God has done for them.

(C) It promotes unity in the church.

(D) It's an opportunity to get to brag on God.

(E) It reinforces to new Christians the advantages of following God and placing faith in Him.

(F) It tells others that you believe in what your dad preaches.

(G) A testimony of salvation is one of the most powerful tools in leading others to Christ. (Share how you received Christ.)

(H) It's an opportunity to publicly say thanks to people who have helped you such as your parents, youth pastor, Sunday school teacher, friends, etc.

(I) It encourages you to live right.

(J) It's a great way to show that you're not ashamed of God or what you believe.

You never know what other people in the church are going through. As a pastor's kid, people will look to you for inspiration, direction, leadership, affirmation, and support. When you are quick to stand and give a testimony you can accomplish all of those things. You know, God has been good to all of us. Sure, there's hard times but there's always somebody who has got it worse. I've gathered much strength over the years through hearing other brothers and sisters in God share their testimonies of how they had hard times but God saw them through. I've also had the privilege of hearing folks in the church say good things about me in their testimonies. It was both embarrassing and flattering.

I've learned how much I liked praise and recognition by church members, so I've tried to return the favor. I've also worked hard not to let these praises be in vain.

There are some "don'ts" involved in giving a testimony. You don't want to defeat the purpose by giving a wrong testimony.

I've heard people get up in church testimony services and talk about how they used to drink, smoke, do drugs, party all night, make millions of dollars and have a different sexual partner every night. They'd go into details about their wild life before becoming a Christian. Sometimes as they were sharing those details I got the opinion that they were bragging about or actually missing their past life. As they spoke, the women would blush and the teens would drool all over themselves.

It also can send the message that others can live like the devil, then, just like that; change. I believe in change and I'm glad when a prodigal son returns home but his past life should stay in the past. We don't need to hear all of the gross details. Most people who get involved in sin are permanently damaged by it. They will either never make it back or they will bear the horrible, permanent scars of regret that always accompanies the life of rebellion and sin. Knowing this, we never want to encourage others to live life in the fast lane of carnality. They might not be as fortunate as you! Some other no-no's of giving a testimony are . . .

(A) Making public confessions. (Use the altar or the pastor's study for counsel.)

(B) Using it as a time to bash others. You will be anti-spiritual.

(C) A testimony should be short and to the point, a few minutes long, a planned thought not a rambling.

(D) Not a time to air complaints or gripes.

(E) Try not to brag on yourself, people will resent this and not be inspired. Brag on God and on others mostly.

(F) Don't key on negative issues. Be positive!!

(G) Don't go into details about your sins. Be vague about it, the church doesn't need intimate details of your life.

(H) Don't preach a sermon.

(I) Don't beat the members of the church. (Remember, you're not the pastor, leave that to your dad.)

(J) Don't be sarcastic or insincere.

These are all just common sense. Give a testimony the next time you have an opportunity. This is a great tool of endearment to your church family. People know you are nervous to speak in public but that's O.K. They'll love you and appreciate you for sharing with them. People who won't testify are people who act ashamed of God or they imply that God has not done anything for them.

"For whosoever shall be ashamed of me and of my words, of him shall the Son of man be ashamed, when he shall come in his own glory, and in his Father's and of the holy angels."

—Luke 9:26

"For I am not ashamed of the gospel of Christ: for it is the power of God unto salvation to every one that believeth; to the Jew first, and also to the Greek."

- Romans 1:16

"Yet if any man suffer as a Christian, let him not be ashamed; but let him glorify God on this behalf."

—I Peter 4:16

7) Go to the altar during every invitation.

I try to go to the altar during every invitation. I do this for several reasons. One. There is something in every sermon that speaks to me. Two. There is a certain amount of humility that is demonstrated when you bow to your knees in front of the church to pray. Sure, you can pray in the pew but I believe that God likes us to humble ourselves before Him. Lots of people never go to the altar because of their pride. They're afraid that others will think they are sinners. (Which they are, we all are!) My grandmother went to a church that wasn't known for it's altar use. They got a new pastor and my dad asked grandma how she liked the new pastor and his family. She replied, "He's real good but his daughter must sure be a wild one." Dad asked, "Why do you say that?" She replied, "Because, she goes to the altar after every service." Dad had to explain to grandma that there are many reasons besides confession for going to the altar. Let me list a few good reasons for going to the altar every service.

(A) To pray for others.

(B) To pray for personal needs.

(C) To pray for the lost in church.

(D) It causes movement to the front of the church during invitation, this helps lost people to come forward, by creating a flow upwards. (In lots of churches the invitation is the time when most of the church slips out the back to go to the bathroom, nursery, outside to talk, etc. This is bad because the invitation is the single most important and serious time of the service! I would hate to cause people to be distracted from going to the altar because I'm going away from it!)

(E) It keeps you humble.

(F) It's a good testimony.

(G) It keeps you on the right path and out of sin.

Don't get me wrong. I'm not talking about showing off your spirituality. Someone said once, "You don't have to have a showy religion for your religion to show." This is very true. Don't be insincere or fake. You don't have to be up front crying and shouting to be effective. If you can't go to the altar and be real then you really do need to hit the altar! Jesus said in the Bible . . .

"Blessed are they that mourn: for they shall be comforted."
—Matthew 5:4

The altar has also been called the "mourner's bench". There is comfort that only comes through prayer. If you can sincerely mourn and cry out to God, He'll hear you and marvelous things can happen. Read Acts 12 for a great story of the power of prayer. Many great men of God will admit that the source of their strength is prayer. Both their own prayers and the prayers from others on their behalf. Use that altar every service! No church can have the power of God until they get the cobwebs out of their altar! God can use you to lead others to better prayer habits, if you frequently hit the altar! A person who is filled with God's marvelous power is one who will frequently fill the altar.

"If my people, which are called by my name, shall humble themselves, and pray, and seek my face, and turn from their wicked ways; then will I hear from heaven, and will forgive their sin, and will heal their land."

—II Chronicles 7:14

"I pray thee, O God, that I may be beautiful within."

—Socrates

8) Go to Christian events.

Youth conferences, pastor fellowships, bus conferences, revivals, etc. are great for you to attend. You will get encouraged by the sermons and you will meet other Christians like yourself. It's a great place to meet friends. I met my wife at a pastor's fellowship. I wasn't really trying to scope for babes, it just kind of happened that way! What better place to meet a good Christian dating prospect than at Christian events? Just something to think about. I know that many times as a P.K. I fell into the faulty belief that we were the only family in the world that believed this way or we were the only family who had a burden for God's work as we do. It was so refreshing to go to Christian events and see that indeed there were thousands who believed just like we did. We weren't alone after all.

Ask your dad if you can accompany him on his trips to preach or attend meetings abroad. I think you'll find it helpful and it's a great way to spend time with your dad. Some of my greatest memories are of going with my dad to revivals and conferences. I got to hear some of the world's greatest preachers, meet some good, godly people, and have good talks with dad going to and from the events. If Christians don't support Christian events, then, who will? Hey, the next time your dad is preaching somewhere ask if you can ride along or if you have a car you might want to surprise him by getting some friends together and showing up to support the meeting. Your dad will love it and so will the host pastor.

9) Don't miss church.

It's a horrible testimony for you to miss church! You must avoid jobs that take you from church. Be sure to do your best to attend all revival services and conferences at your church as well. God has commanded us to be faithful to church. The Bible says...

> "*Not forsaking the assembling of ourselves together, as the manner of some is; but exhorting one another, and so much the more, as ye see the day approaching. For if we sin willfully after that we have received the knowledge of the truth, there remaineth no more sacrifice for sins. But a certain fearful looking for of judgment and fiery indignation, which shall devour the adversaries. He that despised Moses' law died without mercy under two or three witnesses: Of how much sorer punishment, suppose ye, shall he be thought worthy, who hath trodden under foot the Son of God, and hath counted the blood of the covenant, wherewith he was sanctified, an unholy thing, and hath done despite unto the Spirit of grace? For we know him that hath said, Vengeance belongeth unto me, I will recompense, saith the Lord. And again, The Lord shall judge his people. It is a fearful thing to fall into the hands of the living God.*"
>
> —Hebrews 10:25-31

It is imperative that a child of God be faithful to church. I think it's a horrible testimony for a P.K. to lay out of church for any reason! You may be thinking that I'm wasting my time to write this but I've been taken aback by the number of times I've gone to many revivals and meetings where the pastor's kids didn't want to come, so, they just stayed home. It saddens and sickens me how many minister's kids do not attend church as they should. It must break God's heart to see the number of "out of church" P.K.'s. Don't you become one of them!

Most P.K.'s don't plan on getting out of church. They just don't plan not to. It happens gradually for most. I heard a story about a P.K. who left home and went to college. His mother made him promise that he'd go to church every Sunday. He assured her that he'd be faithful. After a few weeks of being on his own some friends asked him to go horseback riding on the upcoming Sunday morning. He at first declined the invitation but through the constant persistence of his friends and the pressure that followed to be his own man, to spread his wings and to broaden his horizons, he reluctantly agreed to accompany them on the excursion. They went to the country and they rented some horses. As they were riding, an old country church nearby began ringing it's church bells to alert the people that church would soon be starting. The P.K. stopped his horse and looked towards the direction of the bells but then continued to ride on. As they went on the bells became more and more faint until they were just barely noticeable. Just then, the P.K. stopped and said, "I must go back while I can still hear the bells!" I know a lot of P.K.'s who have been out so long, they no longer hear the bells calling them back. Don't let this happen to you. Not only will it affect you but it will affect your children and their children to be raised in a godless world. Failure to plan is planning to fail, so plan to be in church to stay.

I hear many minister's kids use the excuse "I don't go to church because my mom and dad made me go." They say this with such conviction and hideous anger and with resentment welled up in every word. Let me say to those who use this as an illegitimate excuse, why don't you find a new lie and excuse for your poor character and self-centered, child-like philosophy. That line is such an overused cliché. I hear P.K.'s use that and it makes me pity them that they are so shallow and fragile. Prototypically it's losers and quitters as well as spoiled rotten simpletons who hide behind such a cowardly and lame excuse as that. I mean come on, your parents make you do a lot of things. I bet they made you take a shower, brush your teeth, clean up your room, eat your dinner, and go to school and I've never heard one person ever say that they'll no longer do these things or even not make their kids do them! I can just hear someone say, "I just don't take showers any more because my parents made me take them as a child." You'd think someone who is making any such claim is crazy or just a little unstable. Well, using that excuse for dropping church out of your life is just as crazy! As a professional counselor, I know that any such claim is just a mask that conceals a much bigger problem, a spiritual problem, an immaturity problem.

A person who despises church or doesn't attend is a person who shows little regard for God or God's will. I can't understand how any P.K. who has seen first hand the power and provision of God and the terror of the Lord could hold God's home with such little regard. God will not and cannot bless your life or your family if you do not obey him. Skipping church will only bring shame and God's terrible wrath on you. It may not show until years later but be not deceived. God is not mocked!

The fact that God loves you and has saved you and that God has been good to you should make you wish to please him with all your might and all your soul. Attending church is among the least of the things you can do to honor and obey God. As a Christian I've always wondered at the marvelous and wonderful love of God! The only thing that is more bewildering than the fact that God could personally and so strongly love me with such an unconditional and undeserved love is the way that man can disregard such love and in many cases hold God in such contempt! To me, that is the greatest wonder of all wonders. All I know is that my parents made me and my two brothers and two sisters go to church and soul winning as children. Now that we are adults, we no longer have to be made to do it. We do it because it's right and because God has been so good to us. Every day I wake up alive, God's been good. As long as I'm breathing His air and living in His world I'm in debt to Him.

The least I can do is go to church and worship Him. Do you realize that if you went to Sunday school and all three services regularly each week that you will average about four and a half hours worth in church per week. What's four and a half hours worth in your life? To me, I can afford it if it means being obedient and faithful. I tell people that I was raised on drugs! I was drug to Sunday school and church at least three times a week and I survived it.

Maybe you are just a weak minded, self centered, bitter person who can't get over being made to do anything. If this is so, then you are in for one long and miserable life. I will pity your wife and kids. As for me and my house, we're just going to fear God and obey His wishes concerning church. Don't get out of church, no matter what!

> *"Remember the Sabbath day, to keep it holy. Six days shalt thou labour, and do all thy work: But the seventh day is the sabbath of the Lord thy God: in it thou shalt not do any work, thou, nor thy son, nor thy daughter, nor thy manservant, nor thy maidservant, nor thy cattle, nor thy stranger that is within thy gates: For in six days the Lord made heaven and earth, the sea, and all that in them is, and rested the seventh day: wherefore the Lord blessed the sabbath day, and hallowed it."*
>
> —Exodus 20:8-11

> *"For the husband is the head of the wife, even as Christ is the head of the church: and he is the saviour of the body. Therefore as the church is subject unto Christ, so let the wives be to their own husbands in every thing. Husbands, love your wives, even as Christ also loved the church, and gave himself for it;"*
>
> —Ephesians 5:23-25

> *"Keep the sabbath day to sanctify it, as the Lord thy God hath commanded thee. Six days thou shalt labour, and do all thy work: But the seventh day is the sabbath of the Lord thy God: in it thou shalt not do any work, thou, nor thy son, nor thy daughter, nor thy manservant, nor thy maidservant, nor thy ox, nor thine ass, nor any of thy cattle, nor thy stranger that is within thy gates; that thy manservant and thy maidservant may rest as well as thou."*
>
> —Deuteronomy 5:12-15

> *"Know therefore that the Lord thy God, he is God, the faithful God, which keepeth covenant and mercy with them that love him and keep his commandments to a thousand gen-*

erations; And repayeth them that hate him to their face, to destroy them: he will not be slack to him that hateth him, he will repay him to his face. Thou shalt therefore keep the commandments, and the statutes, and the judgments, which I command thee this day, to do them."

—Deuteronomy 7:9-11

"The fear of the Lord is the beginning of wisdom: and the knowledge of the holy is understanding."

—Proverbs 9:10

10) Always bring your Bible, a pen, and notebook to church.

Learn to take notes and follow along with the preaching in your Bible. You will learn so much more if you come to church prepared to learn. If you write notes on the sermons you hear, you will be able to remember it much more clearly. With every sermon preached there is some knowledge that will make you a better person. Knowledge is what will make you more apt for success. Don't let all that knowledge pass you by and go unnoticed. Those sermons and Bible studies can make you a better student, athlete, son / daughter, brother / sister, husband / wife, parent, worker, friend, and just an all around better person. Come to church ready to learn, listen, and take notes! As a young preacher, those thousands of notes I took as a young person are so valuable to me now. Some day they will prove useful to you also. It may be during a family crisis, a counseling session with your child, answering a Bible question at work, or just during one of those many days when you just need a little "pick me up" in your spiritual life.

A great price was paid by countless martyrs for us to be able to have our own copy of the word of God in English. (Read the Foxes Book of Martyrs for more info on this subject.) I'm amazed at how many church members come to church without their Bible! I've seen countless young people sit in church with their Bibles shut and their pens silent. What a great waste this is. Develop this good habit now and you'll find church to be much more enjoyable and profitable for you, because with knowledge is power.

"Receive my instruction, and not silver; and knowledge rather than choice gold. For wisdom is better than rubies; and all the things that may be desired are not to be compared to it.."
—Proverbs 8:10 & 11

"Hear instruction, and be wise, and refuse it not. Blessed is the man that heareth me, watching daily at my gates, waiting at the posts of my doors. For whoso findeth me findeth life, and shall obtain favour of the Lord. But he that sinneth against me wrongeth his own soul; all they that hate me love death."

—Proverbs 8:33-36

11) Have a daily personal Bible study and devotion time.

You must have a time that is set aside to study the Bible and worship God daily. Nothing can take the place of personal Bible study and prayer! It is essential for your personal growth, your walk with God, your development as a person, and the dispensation of God's glorious power in your life. I must admit that this is a hard habit to develop. The devil wants you to avoid at all costs reading your Bible and prayer. He'll see to it that everything in the world will happen during your Bible study time to keep you from having it. One problem that I always noticed is the "sleep factor". This is the fact that every night or morning when I'd try to read my Bible I'd get so drowsy, I could hardly hold my head up! More than once I woke up the next morning with my Bible still sitting on the pillow next to me as I fell asleep during the middle of reading it. I used to hear sermons on this topic where I was instructed to read my Bible every night before I went to bed. The idea being that the last thing you should think about is God as you drift off to sleep. There is much credibility to such an idea. However, it didn't work for me, I am such a night owl and I do most of my work in the evening that it made me real inconsistent in my devotion time. I've heard other preachers teach that you must do it first thing in the morning so that you can start the day off right. I must say that there is a lot of wisdom in that teaching but again, for me it just didn't work. As a night owl, I've never been known for getting up extremely early. I get up early because I have to not because I enjoy it. My wife is a early bird.

She gets up each morning happy and singing "Good morning, Lord". I, on the other hand, wake up and say "Good Lord, it's morning already?" I had to learn what worked for me. I study from 11:00 a.m. to 12:00 p.m. most days. That is the time that I am most alert and I get the most out of it. You may prefer other times and that's OK. Do what works for you. Let me give you some practical suggestions to help you enrich your devotion time.

(A) Set a specific time to do it.

(B) Have a systematic method of Bible study.
Note: I've always found the "Through the Bible in a Year" program to be excellent. It is included at the end of this chapter.

(C) Study your Bible to learn it, not just to read it.

(D) Find somewhere where you can be undisturbed and focused during you devotions.
Note: Avoid doing it in a room where the TV or radio is on or where people are talking. This will limit your distractions.

(E) Begin your study and conclude it with prayer.

(F) Have a prayer list.
Note: Include family, friends, object needs, sick, America, etc.

(G) Begin every prayer with a few moments of praise to God for his goodness and for his greatness. It's also a great time to thank God for answered prayers. (Praise and thanks gives you better chances for future answered prayers!)

(H) Pray for God's power and direction in your life.

(I) Pray for others first, yourself last.

(J) Don't replace the Bible with other Christian books.
Note: Stay with the Old Book! It's irreplaceable. Many

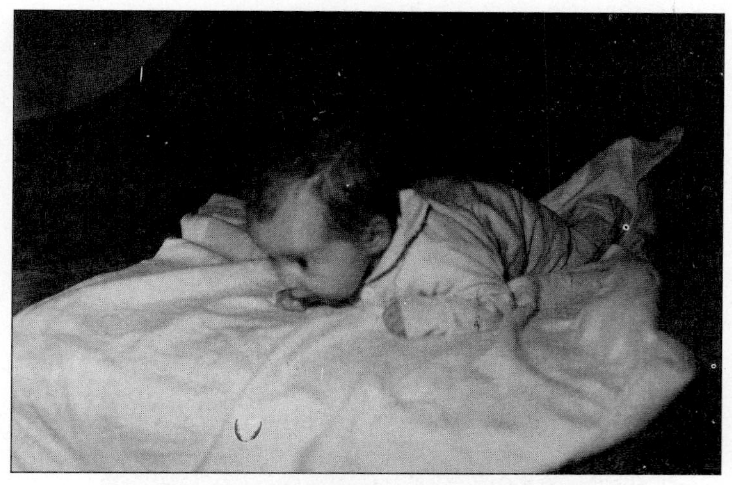

Russell Glenn Riggs as an infant.

My mother, sister and I on "Old Fashioned Day" in 1974.

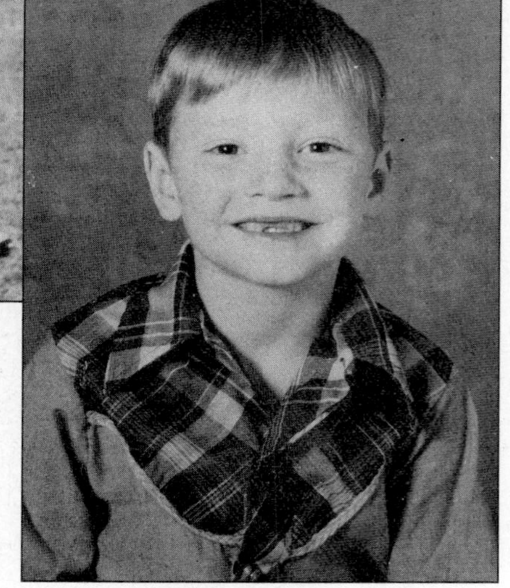

This picture of me was taken during my "Opie Taylor" years.

Hot Springs Baptist Temple's new home.

Hot Springs Baptist Temple in the early years.

A straight on view of the revolving stage at Hot Springs Baptist Temple in 1980.

The Riggs family in 1983.

Fastest growing church in the state of Arkansas!

Baptist Temple growth rapid

If friendliness and commitment are two keys to the growth of a business, the members of Hot Springs Baptist Temple could teach business people a lot about success.

Organized on June 20, 1977, the temple has its own school and a new college, and recently was honored as having the fastest growing Sunday School for 1980 in the state by the International Sunday School Convention of Detroit, Mich.

One of the reasons for the Temple's phenomenal growth are its pastor, Rev. Glenn C. Riggs, and Glenn R. Lewis, associate pastor, who met in 1969 at Walnut Ridge's Southern Baptist College.

"I felt the Lord wanted us to be a team," said Riggs. Lewis went on to California while Riggs pastored Bethabara Baptist Church in Lake City, then Grand Avenue Baptist in Hot Springs. "We left there in August, 1976, to pastor in Rogers, then organized the Baptist Temple here," he added.

The Temple is at 516 Third St., where First Church of the Nazarene was located. It was organized in October, 1977. It now is a member of the Hot Springs Chamber of Commerce, and has the Hot Springs Christian Academy for five-year-olds in kindergarten through twelfth grade.

"We advertise heavily," said Riggs, but the 31-year-old minister doesn't attribute that to the church's growth. "It's like trotline fishing. You can put in the hook and wait, or you can put out a trotline and bring in the fish. Christ said we are to be fishers of men."

The average attendance in June, 1977, for the Temple's Sunday School was 19; by November it was 149, a year later 268, followed the next year by 301 and last month was up to 643. The reason, he said, is simple.

John True, left, presents the Sunday School Growth Award for Arkansas to Pastor Glenn C. Riggs, right, during services at Hot Springs Baptist Temple, 516 Third Street. With them is Glenn R. Lewis.

"We have about 50 people visit each Thursday, and our Ladies Association of Christian Evangelists, headed by Marilyn Geeo, visit on Saturdays,' Riggs said, adding: "We're very aggressive in visiting people."

But he also expressed belief in friendliness, commitment to evangelism and making everyone feel welcome. "We mean that," he said.

A native of Marmaduke, where he graduated from high school in 1967, Riggs attended Southern Baptist College, Arkansas State University in Jonesboro and Ouachita Baptist University at Arkadelphia. He received a Bachelor of Christian Education degree and is working on a Masters degree through the Arkansas Bible Seminary.

He serves as president of the Arkansas Christian School Association and is an executive board member of the American Association of Christian Schools. He and his wife, Carolyn, have four children—Christy, 11, Rusty, 10, and twins Sammy and Danny, 8.

Me at 14 years old. Check out the leather tie!

This picture was taken on our first day in Hawaii.

Our first service at Windward Baptist Temple in Kailua, HI in 1985.

A Sunday morning at Windward Baptist Temple.

The 1988 Hawaii State Champs. I am on the far right.

Dad and I enjoying one of our favorite pastimes.

My mom and dad, Glenn and Carolyn Riggs.

The Riggs family in 1990.

Oh Happy Day!

Christy and I on our honeymoon in 1996.

Brother Isaac and I preaching in India in 1999.

Christian school students make this mistake because they have to read so many other Christian books, they replace the Bible with them. Inspirational books are great but not as a Bible replacement. Those books are to the Bible what vitamins are to food. Just a supplement not a replacement.

"But continue thou in the things which thou hast learned and hast been assured of, knowing of whom thou hast learned them; And that from a child thou hast known the holy scriptures, which are able to make thee wise unto salvation through faith which is in Christ Jesus. All scripture is given by inspiration of God, and is profitable for doctrine, for reproof, for correction, for instruction in righteousness: That the man of God may be perfect, throughly furnished unto all good works."

—II Timothy 3:14-17

"Hear therefore, O Israel, and observe to do it; that it may be well with thee, and that ye may increase mightily, as the Lord God of thy fathers hath promised thee, in the land that floweth with milk and honey. Hear, O Israel: The Lord our God is one Lord: And thou shalt love the Lord thy God with all thine heart, and with all thy soul. and with all thy might. And these words, which I command thee this day, shall be in thine heart. And thou shalt teach them diligently unto thy children, and thou shalt talk of them when thou sittest in thine house, and when thou walkest by the way, and when thou liest down, and when thou risest up. And thou shalt bind them for a sign upon thine hand, and they shall be as frontlets between thine eyes. And thou shalt write them upon the posts of thy house, and on thy gates."

—Deuteronomy 6:3-9

"Thy word is a lamp unto my feet, and a light unto my path."

—Psalms 119:105

"Working for God can never replace spending time loving God."

— Dr. Glenn Riggs

12) Find a pastor that you respect for spiritual counsel.

As a P.K. you will most likely have a pastor who doubles as a dad. Most of the time he can help you with problems in your life as most godly parents can. However, there will be times when you may want to seek counsel by someone other than dad. There are some times when you will require counsel and you may not feel comfortable going to see dad. When this happens you will need a man or woman who you trust to guide you. I have several pastors who I've consulted over the years for counsel and I've valued those men and their opinions. It's helped me a lot. My dad was my biggest influence but sometimes my needs called for outside help.

A principal or youth pastor can also serve as a great help in the area of counsel. I had a wonderful principal, Dr. Glenn Lewis, who was a big help to me over the years. He's in heaven now but I can still remember his words of wisdom. I also had a very wise youth pastor, Bro. Lance Laird, who still serves as a strong and stable source of advice for me. Be careful going to church members for counsel and be careful who influences you. Dr. Jack Hyles once said, "Anybody who influences you, influences all that you influence." Your counselor needs to be a person of character, a godly example, and a person who you trust and respect.

> "*Without counsel purposes are disappointed: but in the multitude of counselors they are established.*"
>
> —Proverbs 15:22

> "*Where no counsel is the people fall: but in the multitude of counselors there is safety.*"
>
> —Proverbs 11:14

> "*The way of a fool is right in his own eyes: but he that hearkeneth unto counsel is wise.*"
>
> —Proverbs 12:15

13) Be careful who you trust with intimate secrets.

Three preachers were out fishing one time. They were having a great time relaxing and getting away from the pressure of the office. As they were fishing one of the preachers spoke up and said, "I have a problem, I've never told anyone before but I have a struggle with cursing. I can't seem to conquer it. When I get mad or stressed out, horrible words just fly out before I can catch them! I'm so ashamed of it and I'm afraid that someday I'll slip up and do it in front of someone. Will you both pray for me?"

After a few minutes of silence the second preacher spoke. He said, "I, too, have a sin that I'm fighting. He went on to say gambling has been my besetting sin. I play the lottery and sometimes when I'm away where no one can see me, I'll play the slot machines! I know it's wrong, I even preach against it. But it just seems to be a habit that I can't break. Will you pray for me?" Then silence filled the air for a while. The two preachers who confessed looked at the third and said, "We've both shared private secrets with you, now, what is your private sin?" He said, "My besetting sin is telling gossip and I can't wait to get off this boat!"

You must be very sure that the person you are confiding private thoughts to is a person that is trustworthy. Things that you don't want told about your family, your friends, and yourself are best not told at all. So many times I learned this the hard way! I told people things thinking I could trust them and then they told everyone! Many times you'll tell people things and they'll keep it silent until they have a falling out with you then they tell all as they now consider you an enemy. I remember once I had a girlfriend that I told some things to that were very private. I thought that I could trust her with anything and I could, until we broke up two years later. Then, she told everything I ever told her, private confessions, statements made purely out of anger, words said about others. She had me! I had to answer a lot of questions over the next few weeks.

The truth is I didn't mean ninety percent of those things and I meant for one hundred percent of them to stay between her and me. I learned a huge lesson from this. Be careful what you say and who you say it to! Some things are just better kept to yourself so that it doesn't become ammunition later. Girlfriends, boyfriends, best friends are not usually the best people to confide in because the secrecy is only as strong as the relationships are. What you would hate to have told later, keep quiet today. Make sure you trust the person to whom you are confiding in. Remember, anything you say, can be repeated and used against you later!

14) Get a vision for your life.

As I counsel young people today I'm astounded at the large number of them who have absolutely no goal for themselves! I mean as far as the future is concerned, they are totally clueless. I've spoke to juniors and seniors in high school and I've asked them what they have chosen for a career and the most common answer is, "Uh, I don't know, I've never really thought about it a whole lot." I think this is a big mistake. Dr. Wendell Evens used to say "Failure to plan is planning to fail." I've never forgotten that statement and I've tried to apply this great truth to my life. As a P.K. you need to live your life with purpose. That means you need to do everything you do for a reason. As a child my dad taught me this early on. I remember one time I did something that got me in hot water with my dad. He called me into his room and told me to sit down in the big high back chair. (A chair that was affectionately named the "Hot Seat" by my brothers and I.) He told me what he was told and asked me if it was true. I sat there looking at my six foot two inch, two hundred pound dad who was obviously not pleased at the allegations and said, "Yes." Then he caught me off guard with the next question. He asked me the dreaded question that every parent asks in times like those, he asked me, "Why did you do this?" As I sat there, the room started spinning, the walls started closing in, I frantically searched for the solution in my head. I was blanking! When suddenly the answer of answers, the card up the sleeve, the age old cure all came to me! I looked my dad right in the eye and said, "I don't know?"

When I said that, to this day, I swear that I saw fire come from dad's eye sockets as he said, "You don't know!!" "Son, if you're going to do wrong, at least, have a reason for it, don't do it because you're just plain dumb." Needless to say I got a spanking and I learned to live my life with purpose. You need to start setting goals for yourself now as a young person. Sure, the goals may change or be altered in time but at least you are heading in a direction and not just blowing in the wind. I had a break in that I answered the call to preach at the early age of eleven years old. From eleven years old on I knew what God wanted me to do, I knew that God wanted me to go to Bible college and learn the old craft of preaching. That helped me set a course for my life that was sure. A lot of doors were opened and closed by God along the way. The "what" of God's will was known but I learned the "where" as I went along. God may not call you into the ministry but that doesn't mean that God has no plan for you. God created you for a purpose.

You are one of a kind. There is no one on the entire planet that is like you. When God made you, He broke the mold and that means that there can never be another that is completely like you. I know that this seems impossible but it's true! God made you unique in every way. He gave you your looks, your eye color, your hair color, your height, your build, your talents, your personality, your humor, your intelligence, your outlook on life, all of this, God gave you to set you apart from every one else. All the little idiosyncrasies that may seem to be flaws are there to give you a personalized identity. Those are the things that make you, you! A lot of the things that you don't like about yourself are the very things that other people recognize you by, they help distinguish you from everybody else.

We all have things that we don't like about ourselves, our weight, our height, the size of our nose, the lack of muscle tone. We wish we were taller or shorter, thinner or more husky. Girls with straight hair wish they had naturally curly hair and those who have naturally curly hair wish they had straight hair! It never ends. Just think, what kind of world it would be if God made us all alike? It's the variety of people that makes life interesting. God made us the way we are on purpose. The Bible says, this means that before you were born, God knew you. Before your mom and dad ever met and fell in love, God knew you. Before God ever created the earth, He knew that He was going to one day create you.

There are no accidents to God, you were not a uh-oh to God. He didn't look down one day and shout, "Wait a minute, hold everything, who is that? How did he get there? Who authorized that person to be born?" Someone said one time, has it ever occurred to you that nothing occurs to God! God is what we call omnipotent, that is Greek for all knowing. God knows all that is happening in your life. He knows you personally and intimately. The Bible says that even the very hairs on your head are numbered! Jesus said that He's so involved with this world that even when one of the countless number of birds falls from the sky, He personally attends the funeral. I'm saying God is a God of complete purpose.

Scientists tell us that there are no two grains of sand that are just alike, there are no two snow flakes that are identical, out of all the fingerprints in the world since the beginning of time no one has ever had a set to match yours. Everybody's retinas are unique and can be used to identify them. If God went through all the trouble to make you a special creation then He must have had a reason for your existence! What is it? Are you fulfilling the purpose that God designed you for? You can never find true prosperity outside of God's purpose for you. Live your life with purpose, God's purpose.

15) Realize your potential.

"God don't sponsor no flops"

—Ethel Waters

The Bible says . . .

"Whatsoever thy hand findeth to do, do it with thy might; for there is no work, nor device, nor knowledge, nor wisdom, in the grave, whither thou goest."

—Ecclesiastes 9:10

It is godly to be a winner! Give one hundred percent in all you do! It does matter if you win or lose! God is a winner. God is a key figure in the battle of the ages - on one side is God and the forces of righteousness, on the other side, is our adversary - the devil and his motley band of loyal followers! The devil started this war when he dared to overthrow his master and creator. Realizing that he could never be successful in his coup de etat, he went after God's children. He lives to hurt, mangle, and destroy the lives of God's greatest creation, man. God has fought him through the ages. He used Moses to defeat Pharaoh, a young boy named David to rock the world of the enormous giant named Goliath. God used Elijah to fight the forces of paganism and John the Baptist picked up the sword to fight the Pharisees. And, let's not forget the greatest victory of all. That dark day Satan hit God with his hardest shot. He entered the body of Judas, one of Jesus' disciples and friends. Judas betrayed Jesus for thirty measly pieces of silver. The guards came and took our Saviour into custody after Judas pinpointed Him with a kiss on the cheek. Then the devil indulged in his finest hour! They took Jesus and stripped him of his robe and put a purple robe on him to mock him. Then they beat Him with a cat o' nine tails, a horrible whip that had nine straps of leather which had pieces of bone or metal embedded in them. With each lash the bone or metal would grab chunks of skin and rip it away. Jesus was struck thirty-nine times with this macabre instrument. Then the Son of God was made to stand trial and the people elected to release a common professional criminal to enjoy freedom and then they chanted, "Crucify Him, Crucify Him, Crucify Him" when the innocent Jesus was presented to them. In the background, the roar of the Lion was growing louder as Satan was having his hey day. Then Jesus was taken and beaten by the soldiers. They spat upon Him. They mocked Him. All the while, Jesus stood silent and the devil smiled with anticipation as Jesus marched down that lonely road with a rugged cross of wood placed across his back. I imagine the devil was prodding Him and leading Him to that place on the Hill called Golgotha, or the place of the skull.

The place where the most horrible, gruesome, inhumane, and painful execution known to Rome was to be executed. They took rusty, jagged, nine-inch long nails and pounded them through His wrists and then through His ankles. With each clang of the hammer, Jesus screamed in agony and the devil cheered with delight. He was so close to victory, he could taste it! Jesus was nailed to the cross, then raised up and suspended between heaven and earth. As the angels wept and anxiously awaited for Jesus to summon them to His rescue, the demons of hell danced around their commander in chief. Then the Son of God lifted His voice and shouted, "It is finished", then He laid down His life and gave up His spirit. The disciples were in shock. The angels stood down and God turned His back as they placed Jesus in the tomb. For three days Jesus stayed there. I can imagine that every morning Satan left his victory party to check up on his prey. He'd ask Death if Jesus was still under his control, Death would say, "I've got it under control, boss". Then Satan would chuckle as he rejoined his evil cohorts in their devious celebration. Then Satan came by on the third morning and found Death laying on the ground. He was bruised and stunned. The Devil said, "What happened?" And Death said, "Boss, don't get mad. I don't know what happened!" Satan yelled, "Where's the Son of God?" Death said, "I had Him, my hands grasped Him tightly but suddenly He slipped right through my hands! He's free! He rose again!" And the Devil sank to his knees and moaned, "No, No, this can't be true. How did this happen? I was so close. I had you, Jesus, I watched you die." Then Satan remembered the voice of his mortal enemy. His mind reflected to that final moment when Jesus declared, "It is finished." Then suddenly Satan understood it clearly. It was not Jesus' life that was finished. It was this war for the souls of man. Jesus said, "This war is finished and Satan, you lose!!" I'm saying that God is a winner. You should be a winner who strives to reach your potential! God fought to win and so should you.

Only giving one hundred percent is reaching your potential! Ten, twenty, thirty, forty, fifty, sixty, seventy, eighty, ninety percent is not reaching your potential. Reaching your potential means that you are doing all you can do, the best you can do to fulfill the purpose that God has for you. Whatever you do, do it with all that is within you! If God's purpose is for you to be a preacher, then be the best preacher you can be. If God calls you to be a plumber, then be a Christian plumber who strives to be the best plumber you can be. Right now you may not know what God's ultimate purpose is for you but one thing you do know is that right now God wants you to be a minister's kid! OK. Then be a minister's kid who does all you can, the best you can do to reach your potential as the child of a man of God. If you must be a P.K. to fulfill God's purpose, then be a good one!

Sometimes you may do all you can do to win and you honestly know that you did all you could to reach your potential but you still lost. Are you wrong because you lost? You're not always wrong. If you lose, then lose with dignity and style. Be graceful in defeat but strive to learn from it. It may be in sports, in school, at work, a personal goal that you set. If failure comes your way, then remember; One failure isn't final. I remember when I was learning to ride a bike. My dad bought me a beautiful red bike for my fifth birthday. I loved it! But there was one problem, I didn't know how to operate it. Dad was from the old school, no son of his was going to have those sissy training wheels on his bike! Dad said, "Boy, come here." I walked over to him and he said, "Get on the bike.", and like a fool I hopped on. He started pushing me around the yard. I was having a blast on my new hot rod machine. Then suddenly dad aimed me down the road. I felt his pace quicken and his grip tighten. I felt my pulse increase as suddenly I felt like a rock being shot by a sling shot. Dad was pushing me. I was just getting used to it when suddenly dad did the unthinkable. He let go! I went out about thirty feet where I then ran out of steam and flopped over. I ate grass and dirt and I was stunned. I swear that I remember suffering from vertigo. I was laying on the ground, glad to be alive, praising God for delivering me from sure demise. I knew that just then I had successfully cheated a vicious death. Suddenly I felt a hand grab me and the bike. Then, suddenly, I was reliving the whole nightmare again! I started crying. My dad looked at me with all the love and mercy he could muster and said, "Boy, get on that bike or I'll give you something to really cry about! I knew it was meet death via belt or go out in a blaze of glory. I realized that I must conquer this machine and do it quickly! Dad and I repeated this process several more times. I hit a tree, a parked car, my dog, then after about the tenth try, dad pushed me and let go and I sailed away, riding the bike! I learned that day a very important lesson. Falling off a bike hurts! I learned that failure and failure and failure equals success eventually! The road to reaching your potential will be paved with failures. Don't let them keep you down, keep getting up and going after it. Every champion has felt the bitter taste of defeat before he felt the sweet kiss of victory.

I read about a young man who was struggling to achieve his dream as a cartoonist. He had some ideas for some cartoon characters and desperately wanted to succeed in that field. He approached several newspaper companies and they all for one reason or another rejected his work. Then one day he went to this certain editor and begged for a chance. The editor looked him in the eye and said, "Look, you're a bright young man. You've got a lot of potential but I don't think this is your ticket. Maybe you should pursue another line of work and put your energies into that." The young man gathered up his sketches and walked out of that office, defeated, discouraged, and tempted to throw the sketches in the trash. As the gloom lifted he said to himself, "I know I can make it." He kept on trying and trying. That young man was named Walter Disney! He became the king of all cartoonists. Every child knows the name of Walt Disney but does anybody know the name of that editor who rejected him? You keep working hard to reach your potential, suck up the losses, and be motivated by your victories.

Second, learn from defeat. Every loss can teach you something if you'll let it. You've only lost if you learned nothing from it. Third, get back up and keep going. Don't let any loss keep you down. My dad told me a story that I've never forgotten. A young lady sat in her room getting ready for the biggest day of her life. It was her wedding day! She had waited for this day all of her life. She put on her gorgeous white dress. Her mom fixed her hair and placed the long veil on her. Her sister did her make up and made her look more beautiful than she ever imagined she could be. One by one the invited guests began to arrive, the preacher, the organ player, the caterer and waiters. All were ready and in place.

The flowers were perfect, the cake was breathtaking and the anticipation hung heavy in the air. This was to be the greatest day of her life. The wedding was to start at 10:00 a.m.

At 9:45 a knock sounded on this excited bride's door. Her mother answered it and was given a note to deliver to her bride-to-be daughter. The young lady looked at the note and was delighted as she recognized the handwriting to be the love of her life, the young groom to whom she had dedicated to spend her whole life with. She expected a last minute love note, but upon opening the envelope she found a cruel, malaise letter explaining that he was not coming and that he was not going to marry her. The stood up bride laid the note down, asked her mother, sister, and all the guests and workers to disassemble and leave her alone. The preacher and her parents tried to console her but to no avail. She said, "Would you please just leave, I wish to be alone." They all left.

She went around the house and broke every clock and placed the hands on 9:45. She left the cake on the table until the rats literally devoured it. She never left her home again and forever forsook society. She died there a few years later, a miserable, wasted life. All because defeat came at 9:45. Has there been a few 9:45's in your life? If so, get up and get over it! Time heals all wounds and God will bring joy to a broken heart once again! One thing that you will face as a P.K. is plenty of defeat but you will have enough victory to keep you going. Reaching your potential is never easy but that is what separates the winners from the losers. If winning was so easy it wouldn't taste so sweet. Before you can enter the promised land, you'll have to journey through the desolate wilderness. If it's God's purpose, then you have the potential to find prosperity in spite of the opposition. Reaching your potential requires some things.

(1) Determination that never ends.

(2) Self motivation.

(3) Self discipline.

(4) The ability to be directed by others (able to be coached)

(5) Goals of achievement.

(6) The ability to learn from mistakes, both yours and others.

(7) A dedication to accept nothing less than your best in all that you do.

(8) A forgiving spirit. Be able to put past failures in the past and leave them there.

(9) The courage to go for your dreams.

(10) Be in the center of God's will, doing your best to complete God's purpose for you.

(11) Pray for God's power to assist you.

(12) Learn from those who inspire you.

(13) Find a mentor.

(14) Realize that God's view of success is not always man's view of success. Gods recipe for success is found only in the Bible.

"Blessed is the man that walketh not in the counsel of the ungodly, nor standeth in the way of sinners, nor sitteth in the seat of the scornful. But his delight is in the law of the Lord; and in his law doth he meditate day and night. And he shall be like a tree planted by the rivers of water, that bringeth forth his fruit in his season; his leaf also shall not wither; and whatsoever he doeth shall prosper. The ungodly are not so; but are like the chaff which the wind driveth away. Therefore the ungodly shall not stand in the judgment, nor sinners in the congregation of the righteous. For the Lord knoweth the way of the righteous; but the way of the ungodly shall perish.

—Psalm 1

(15) Don't ever, ever quit!

I wonder how many times you've quit when success was just inches away? I read about an archeologist who lived in the 1920's. He'd done some research on a tomb of a great Egyptian king who possessed great wealth. Legend had it that when he died, all of his wealth was placed in the tomb with him. The young archeologist knew if he could locate and excavate that tomb he'd be rich beyond his wildest dreams. He presented his research to some financial sponsors who elected to award him with a grant to search for this elusive fortune. He pinpointed where he thought it was and they began to excavate in the desert sand.

For five long years they dug and searched. After such a long time of looking with no results his grant ran out. He returned to America but his heart remained in Egypt. Forty years later, he once again raised a grant to search and recover this vast fortune. He knew he had to be right! He returned to the exact same spot that he abandoned forty years earlier. They dug about ten feet into the desert sand, when he uncovered the tomb and fortune that sent him on this odyssey forty-five years ago. When he saw it, he went stark raving mad! He was placed in an asylum when all he kept mumbling over and over was, "I was so close, so close, I was so close!!" This illustrates a lot of us on a smaller scale of course. Many times we quit when we're so close to reaching our potential. Hang in there until the end.

Through the Bible in a Year!

The order in which the schedule lists the books is not the order in which they occur in the Bible, but is a chronological arrangement. The poetic and prophetic books of the Old Testament are inserted in the historical books at about the point in the narrative where they are thought to have been written. In like manner the epistles of the New Testament are inserted in the narrative of the book of Acts. While there is some difference of opinion as to details, the chronological arrangement used here is acceptable to leading conservative Bible scholars.

Through the Bible in a Year!					
January		February		March	
Day	Scripture	Day	Scripture	Day	Scripture
1	Genesis 1-2	1	Exodus 14-17	1	Deuteronomy 4-6
2	Genesis 3-5	2	Exodus 18-20	2	Deuteronomy 7-9
3	Genesis 6-9	3	Exodus 21-24	3	Deuteronomy 10-12
4	Genesis 10-11	4	Exodus 25-27	4	Deuteronomy 13-16
5	Genesis 12-15	5	Exodus 28-31	5	Deuteronomy 17-19
6	Genesis 16-19	6	Exodus 32-34	6	Deuteronomy 20-22
7	Genesis 20-22	7	Exodus 35-37	7	Deuteronomy 23-25
8	Genesis 23-26	8	Exodus 38-40	8	Deuteronomy 26-28
9	Genesis 27-29	9	Leviticus 1-4	9	Deuteronomy 29-31
10	Genesis 30-32	10	Leviticus 5-7	10	Deuteronomy 32-34
11	Genesis 33-36	11	Leviticus 8-10	11	Joshua 1-3
12	Genesis 37-39	12	Leviticus 11-13	12	Joshua 4-6
13	Genesis 40-42	13	Leviticus 14-16	13	Joshua 7-9
14	Genesis 43-46	14	Leviticus 17-19	14	Joshua 10-12
15	Genesis 47-50	15	Leviticus 20-23	15	Joshua 13-15
16	Job 1-4	16	Leviticus 24-27	16	Joshua 16-18
17	Job 5-7	17	Numbers 1-3	17	Joshua 19-21
18	Job 8-10	18	Numbers 4-6	18	Joshua 22-24
19	Job 11-13	19	Numbers 7-10	19	Judges 1-4
20	Job 14-17	20	Numbers 11-14	20	Judges 5-8
21	Job 18-20	21	Numbers 15-17	21	Judges 9-12
22	Job 21-24	22	Numbers 18-20	22	Judges 13-15
23	Job 25-27	23	Numbers 21-24	23	Judges 16-18
24	Job 28-31	24	Numbers 25-27	24	Judges 19-21
25	Job 32-34	25	Numbers 28-30	25	Ruth 1-4
26	Job 35-37	26	Numbers 31-33	26	I Samuel 1-3
27	Job 38-42	27	Numbers 34-36	27	I Samuel 4-7
28	Exodus 1-4	28	Deuteronomy 1-3	28	I Samuel 8-10
29	Exodus 5-7			29	I Samuel 11-13
30	Exodus 8-10			30	I Samuel 14-16
31	Exodus 11-13			31	I Samuel 17-20

Through the Bible in a Year!

Day	April Scripture	Day	May Scripture	Day	June Scripture
1	I Samuel 21-24	1	Psalms 61-63	1	Proverbs 1-3
2	I Samuel 25-28	2	Psalms 64-66	2	Proverbs 4-7
3	I Samuel 29-31	3	Psalms 67-69	3	Proverbs 8-11
4	II Samuel 1-4	4	Psalms 70-72	4	Proverbs 12-14
5	II Samuel 5-8	5	Psalms 73-75	5	Proverbs 15-18
6	II Samuel 9-12	6	Psalms 76-78	6	Proverbs 19-21
7	II Samuel 13-15	7	Psalms 79-81	7	Proverbs 22-24
8	II Samuel 16-18	8	Psalms 82-84	8	Proverbs 25-28
9	II Samuel 19-21	9	Psalms 85-87	9	Proverbs 29-31
10	II Samuel 22-24	10	Psalms 88-90	10	Ecclesiastes 1-3
11	Psalms 1-3	11	Psalms 91-93	11	Ecclesiastes 4-6
12	Psalms 4-6	12	Psalms 94-96	12	Ecclesiastes 7-9
13	Psalms 7-9	13	Psalms 97-99	13	Ecclesiastes 10-12
14	Psalms 10-12	14	Psalms 100-102	14	Songs 1-4
15	Psalms 13-15	15	Psalms 103-105	15	Songs 5-8
16	Psalms 16-18	16	Psalms 106-108	16	I Kings 5-7
17	Psalms 19-21	17	Psalms 109-111	17	I Kings 8-10
18	Psalms 22-24	18	Psalms 112-114	18	I Kings 11-13
19	Psalms 25-27	19	Psalms 115-118	19	I Kings 14-16
20	Psalms 28-30	20	Psalms 119	20	I Kings 17-19
21	Psalms 31-33	21	Psalms 120-123	21	I Kings 20-22
22	Psalms 34-36	22	Psalms 124-126	22	II Kings 1-3
23	Psalms 37-39	23	Psalms 127-129	23	II Kings 4-6
24	Psalms 40-42	24	Psalms 130-132	24	II Kings 7-10
25	Psalms 43-45	25	Psalms 133-135	25	II Kings 11-14:20
26	Psalms 46-48	26	Psalms 136-138	26	Joel 1-3
27	Psalms 49-51	27	Psalms 139-141	27	II Kings 14:21-25 Jonah 1-4
28	Psalms 52-54	28	Psalms 142-144	28	II Kings 14:26-29 Amos 1-3
29	Psalms 55-57	29	Psalms 145-147	29	Amos 4-6
30	Psalms 58-60	30	Psalms 148-150	30	Amos 7-9
		31	I Kings 1-4		

Through the Bible in a Year!

July Day	July Scripture	August Day	August Scripture	September Day	September Scripture
1	II Kings 15-17	1	II Kings 20-21	1	II Chronicles 4-6
2	Hosea 1-4	2	Zephaniah 1-3	2	II Chronicles 7-9
3	Hosea 5-7	3	Habakkuk 1-3	3	II Chronicles 10-13
4	Hosea 8-10	4	II Kings 2-25	4	II Chronicles 14-16
5	Hosea 11-14	5	Obadiah Jeremiah 1-2	5	II Chronicles 17-19
6	II Kings 18-19	6	Jeremiah 3-5	6	II Chronicles 20-22
7	Isaiah 1-3	7	Jeremiah 6-8	7	II Chronicles 23-25
8	Isaiah 4-6	8	Jeremiah 9-12	8	II Chronicles 26-29
9	Isaiah 7-9	9	Jeremiah 13-16	9	II Chronicles 30-32
10	Isaiah 10-12	10	Jeremiah 17-20	10	II Chronicles 33-36
11	Isaiah 13-15	11	Jeremiah 21-23	11	Ezekiel 1-3
12	Isaiah 16-18	12	Jeremiah 24-26	12	Ezekiel 4-7
13	Isaiah 19-21	13	Jeremiah 27-29	13	Ezekiel 8-11
14	Isaiah 22-24	14	Jeremiah 30-32	14	Ezekiel 12-14
15	Isaiah 25-27	15	Jeremiah 33-36	15	Ezekiel 15-18
16	Isaiah 28-30	16	Jeremiah 37-39	16	Ezekiel 19-21
17	Isaiah 31-33	17	Jeremiah 40-42	17	Ezekiel 22-24
18	Isaiah 34-36	18	Jeremiah 43-46	18	Ezekiel 25-27
19	Isaiah 37-39	19	Jeremiah 47-49	19	Ezekiel 28-30
20	Isaiah 40-42	20	Jeremiah 50-52	20	Ezekiel 31-33
21	Isaiah 43-45	21	Lamentations 1-5	21	Ezekiel 34-36
22	Isaiah 46-48	22	I Chronicles 1-3	22	Ezekiel 37-39
23	Isaiah 49-51	23	I Chronicles 4-6	23	Ezekiel 40-42
24	Isaiah 52-54	24	I Chronicles 7-9	24	Ezekiel 43-45
25	Isaiah 55-57	25	I Chronicles 10-13	25	Ezekiel 46-48
26	Isaiah 58-60	26	I Chronicles 14-16	26	Daniel 1-3
27	Isaiah 61-63	27	I Chronicles 17-19	27	Daniel 4-6
28	Isaiah 64-66	28	I Chronicles 20-23	28	Daniel 7-9
29	Micah 1-4	29	I Chronicles 24-26	29	Daniel 10-12
30	Micah 5-7	30	I Chronicles 27-29	30	Esther 1-3
31	Nahum 1-3	31	II Chronicles 1-3		

Through the Bible in a Year!

October		November		December	
Day	**Scripture**	**Day**	**Scripture**	**Day**	**Scripture**
1	Esther 4-7	1	Luke 14-17	1	Romans 5-8
2	Esther 8-10	2	Luke 18-21	2	Romans 9-11
3	Ezra 1-4	3	Luke 22-24	3	Romans 12-16
4	Haggai 1-2 Zechariah 1-2	4	John 1-3	4	Acts 20:3-22
5	Zechariah 3-6	5	John 5-6	5	Acts 23-25
6	Zechariah 7-10	6	John 7-10	6	Acts 26-28
7	Zechariah 11-14	7	John 11-13	7	Ephesians 1-3
8	Ezra 5-7	8	John 14-17	8	Ephesians 4-6
9	Ezra 8-10	9	John 18-21	9	Philippians 1-4
10	Nehemiah 1-3	10	Acts 1-2	10	Colossians 1-4
11	Nehemiah 4-6	11	Acts 3-5	11	Hebrews 1-4
12	Nehemiah 7-9	12	Acts 6-9	12	Hebrews 5-7
13	Nehemiah 10-13	13	Acts 10-12	13	Hebrews 8-10
14	Malachi 1-4	14	Acts 13-14	14	Hebrews 11-13
15	Matthew 1-4	15	James 1-2	15	Philemon I Peter 1-2
16	Matthew 5-7	16	James 3-5	16	I Peter 3-5
17	Matthew 8-11	17	Galatians 1-3	17	II Peter 1-3
18	Matthew 12-15	18	Galatians 4-6	18	I Timothy 1-3
19	Matthew 16-19	19	Acts 15-18:11	19	I Timothy 4-6
20	Matthew 20-22	20	I Thessalonians 1-5	20	Titus 1-3
21	Matthew 23-25	21	II Thessalonians 1-3 Acts 18:12-19:10	21	II Timothy 1-4
22	Matthew 26-28	22	I Corinthians 1-4	22	I John 1-2
23	Mark 1-3	23	I Corinthians 5-8	23	I John 3-5
24	Mark 4-6	24	I Corinthians 9-12	24	II John, III John Jude
25	Mark 7-10	25	I Corinthians 13-16	25	Revelation 1-3
26	Mark 11-13	26	Acts 19:11-20:1 II Corinthians 1-3	26	Revelation 4-6
27	Mark 14-16	27	II Corinthians 4-6	27	Revelation 7-9
28	Luke 1-3	28	II Corinthians 7-9	28	Revelation 10-12
29	Luke 4-6	29	II Corinthians 10-13	29	Revelation 13-15
30	Luke 7-9	30	Acts 20:2 Romans 1-4	30	Revelation 16-18
31	Luke 10-13			31	Revelation 19-22

4
Things I've Found

"*Happy is the man that findeth wisdom, and the man that getteth understanding.*"

—Proverbs 3:13

When I was a little boy I remember a popular slogan that swept through the churches of America. It was the catch phrase, "I found it". It was on billboards, bumper stickers, book covers, lapel pins, pencils and buttons. When you'd wear the button people would read it and be compelled to ask what it is that you found. Then there would be a perfect opportunity to tell them how you found joy, happiness, and completion through finding the Lord in your life! Many people got saved using this catchy phrase.

As I've lived my life there are some things that I've found. Things that have changed my life in one way or another. Things that have helped me to find victory in my Christian life.

1. I've found that I have a sworn enemy.

"*Be sober, be vigilant; because your adversary the devil, as a roaring lion, walketh about, seeking whom he may devour.*"

—I Peter 5:8

"*Ye are of your father the devil, and the lusts of your father ye will do. He was a murderer from the beginning, and abode not in the truth, because there is no truth in him. When he speaketh a lie, he speaketh of his own; for he is a liar, and the father of it."*

—John 8:44

The Bible says that the devil is as a roaring lion who wants to devour me and destroy my life at every turn. The lion is an animal that is known for being the king of the jungle. It's a huge cat that is extremely strong and has a terrible roar. It's not known for it's speed as the cheetah is, so it has to depend upon the ambush tactic to capture it's prey. I've been told that it will hide in the thick tall grass where it blends in perfectly. An unsuspecting caribou will graze right up to it. The lion will pounce and let out a mighty roar that can be heard up to one mile away. This roar is said to be so powerful that it stuns the prey and confuses it. This causes it to freeze up and the slower but powerful lion can sink his razor sharp claws and teeth into it. Once he's grasped it, it's all she wrote for the poor caribou. It will be torn to shreds by the roaring lion.

It's no accident that God used the lion to describe our enemy, the Devil. The Devil works this way. He'll ambush an unsuspecting, uncareful Christian who is lagging behind or away from the pack (the Church), and/or spiritually weak. I've seen the bloody mess he's made out of many Christians. He's sunk his claws and teeth into them and ripped them to shreds. I've seen the wrecked homes that his drugs, alcohol, and adultery have produced. I've seen the teen age girls who have become women at fourteen and fifteen because they are pregnant by a boy who couldn't care less about them. I've seen teen age boys sell their body to sleazy older men so they could buy some more poison to shoot into their collapsing veins. I've seen mothers cry bitter tears over the massacred life of a child that they used to nurse and hold so dear. I've gone to the homes of scenes like these. In the faint distance I've heard the lion roar as he struts away with a belly that's full and the satisfaction of another notch on his still smoking gun.

The word Devil literally means adversary. The Devil is our sworn enemy. He's a trickster and a con man. A master of illusions. He was the most powerful and beautiful angel that God created. His style is beauty. Every proposal he makes is shrouded in enticing secrecy. He is the king of lies, the sultan of broken dreams, the advocate of pain. No one has ever engaged the Devil and been made better through him. He only knows how to take and deceive. I've found him to be no good and always against me. He and his band of heavenly rejects fight every good decision I try to make. They are forever trying to sway me from the road that I must travel. If he could gut me and leave me drowning in my blood tonight, he would surely do it! He would do it to you also! He is forever our foe.

2. I've found a personal friend in Jesus.

> "*A man that hath friends must shew himself friendly: and there is a friend that sticketh closer than a brother.*"
>
> —Proverbs 18:24

I've been blessed in my life with some dear friends. James and Jensen Payte, Phil Graham, Mike Carringer, John Aquino, Matt Gibbs, Larry Stephen, Greg Sneathern, these names are truly dear to me. I've spent good times in my life with these guys. I share many fond memories with them. It's a great thing to have a close friend. A comrade, someone to share dreams and secrets with. In my life friends have come and gone. There are miles between us. We are busy trying to keep pace with a constantly changing world. Sadly, our relationships aren't what they used to be. As I've grown older, I've discovered that I have a friend. A friend that is like no other! One who is always there, one who never lets me down, one who is never too busy for me, one who always wants what's best for me and one who loves me even when I know I don't deserve his love. That friend is Jesus! I know it sounds like such a cliche or like a lyric from an old hymn, but as I've grown in the Lord, I've grown to know the Lord as a personal friend.

I guess I really realized just how much I needed to be close to Jesus on September 19, 1995. It was exactly 2:47 p.m. according to my gold watch that is frozen on that day and time. It was a day like any other when I woke up that morning. I had several errands to run before work and a schedule that included taking a group of teens to Berean Baptist Church in Ocala, Florida where my dad and Dr. Johnny Pope were going to preach that evening. I went out to my car that morning and saw that I was running on empty. I decided that since I had such a busy day I would just take my motorcycle. It was a beautiful Florida day so I was excited about riding my bike. I went through my day as usual. I taught my classes, worked out, had lunch at my mother's house and coached basketball practice.

I cut basketball practice short and left at 2:30 to go home and get a shower and put on a suit. I had to be back at the church by 5:00 to take the bus to Ocala. It was on my way home that my life was forever changed. As I was riding my bike I went into a curve. They had been working on the road and there was sand everywhere. In Florida sand is called "Florida Ice" because it can be very slick when it accumulates on the road. When I hit the curve and sand my bike began to slide. Out of control I went catapulting into the other lane. I remember feeling the bike slide. I looked down and saw my back tire, then I looked up about 5 feet in front of me was a school bus! I closed my eyes and turned my head. I thought, well, this is it Rusty. You've lived your last day. You are a dead man. I heard a loud thunderous crash. A noise one could never forget. A noise that has awaken me many nights since, as it sounds off in my dreams. Every thing then went black and it was as if I was floating. Then I felt a jarring blow as I tumbled down the road. I fully expected to see the face of God when I opened my horror filled eyes. When I came to rest, to my amazement I was alive. I even thought that I had escaped serious injury. My helmet was twisted to the side which blinded me. I was disoriented and I heard a loud noise in my head that sounded like a tornado alarm.

I tried to get my helmet off but my hands wouldn't work right. It was then that I knew it was bad. When I finally looked down I saw that my left arm was snapped in two. I had a bloody stump staring back at me and some skin holding my arm together. My right wrist was shattered and it looked like I had a plum stuck under the skin of my wrist. My left leg looked like a shark had bit a chunk out of it and my right knee cap was knocked to the side of my leg. I had a broken hip and my shoulder was fractured. There I was a healthy twenty-five year old man. That morning I was 10 feet tall and bullet proof, now I'm a mangled mass of flesh laying in a five feet diameter circle of blood. They tell me that I stopped breathing and they had to do CPR on me as they air-lifted me to the Orlando Regional Hospital. I'll spare you all the details of the next few months. I was paralyzed from the waist down for two months and I had seven surgeries over the next two years to fix my arms and other injuries. I had a lot of support during that time from friends and family. I had to move back in to my parent's home to be rehabilitated. My mother had to shave me, feed me, and basically take care of me like a baby. She had to clean and dress my grotesque wounds daily and put up with the emotions that the drugs caused me to go through. Anger, depression, anxiety, and hopelessness. My dad had to bathe me and help me in very awkward situations. I'll never forget how my parents were there during that special time.

But the greatest thing for me during that time was I really discovered a personal relationship with Jesus. I've never prayed like I did during those two years. I spent a lot of time alone and unable to do anything but talk to God. I know He was with me. After I went through this I have a new understanding of the twenty-third Psalm. I wouldn't wish this on anybody but I know it helped me see Jesus and come to really know him. Today, I can truly sing "What a friend we have in Jesus, all our pains and griefs to bear!" I hope you'll find Jesus as your personal friend.

3. I've found the will of God as my life's purpose.

> *"Commit thy works unto the LORD, and thy thoughts shall be established."*
>
> —Proverbs 16:3

It's great to have a purpose for living! I've found that in the will of God there is joy unspeakable, success that is lasting and fulfilling. There is nothing like the will of God! Satan has a will for you also,but it's not the same. Satan's will is what's best for him. God's will is what's best for you. It's a relief to know that God holds my tomorrow and that it's not up to me. If I follow God then prosperity is guaranteed. I'm glad that I found the will of God in my life. Have you?

4. I've found the Holy Spirit as my guide.

When I was in India I was so glad that I was not alone in such a strange, huge place! Everything was different. They drove on the opposite side of the road and with different rules. They had strange laws and they spoke a language that I did not understand! I was so glad that Bro. Isaac and Bro. Dan were with me. They took care of me and taught me how to live in India. They were my guides. Where they sent me, I went, where they led, I followed. When they instructed, I listened.

The Holy Spirit is our guide in this life. He can lead you to the will of God. You must find him as your guide. Prayer and Bible study can increase his power in your life. You must learn to trust Him to be the leader, where He sends, Go! Where He leads, follow!

Some years ago a plane that was almost entirely intact was discovered in the Sahara desert. Upon examination, it was learned that it was a U.S. Air Force bomber of World War II vintage. On the fuselage was the name: *Lady Be Good.* The discovery of the craft revealed a great mystery of the war. What happened? Upon examination they discovered that the ship had left to run a mission to North Africa and was never heard from again! The plane was found some four hundred miles past it's destination. When they checked the instruments they found them all to still be in working order and accurate. They surmise that the *Lady Be Good* had overshot it's goal because it was caught in an high altitude air current that doubled its speed without the pilot being aware of it. The pilot knew how long the flight normally took and didn't trust the instruments which said that they'd arrived. He kept flying until he ran out of gas and crash landed in the Sahara Desert.

A few miles away from the plane they unearthed the skeletal remains of the crew. They lost their way and their lives because they didn't trust their instruments. As a child of God we have instruments to help us follow the Holy Spirit. They are . . .

(A) The Word of God. Psalms 119:105.

(B) Prayer. Jeremiah 33:3; Proverbs 3:1-7.

(C) Christian counsel. Proverbs 13:20; Proverbs 11:14.

1. Parents. Proverbs 13:1; Proverbs 4:10.

2. Pastor. Proverbs 9:7-9.

3. Youth Pastor.

4. Sunday School Teacher.

Learn to trust the Holy Spirit and you'll find that he'll never lead you astray! May you find these things in your life.

"Shew me thy ways, O Lord; teach me thy paths. Lead me in thy truth, and teach me: for thou art the God of my salvation; on thee do I wait all the day."

—Psalm 25:4, 5

5

Is It Really That Bad?

As I counsel many minister's kids, I've noted that the general attitude is one of persecution. All of the P.K.'s viewed themselves as modern day martyrs. And I must admit, I was also guilty of thinking that way. For many years I played the horrible victim, I would whine about how hard it is to be a P.K. and how no one understands the realities of it. My sinful nature told me that I was the only one who had it so bad. Sadly, I was sometimes guilty of blaming God and the church for all my problems! I felt that it was all related, somehow to the fact that I was a P.K. and that there was more pressure placed on me, somehow.

As I've grown up and matured, God has helped me to see some things through his eyes. In retrospect, I don't think I had it so bad. I know that others had it much worse. This truth was made real to me on a trip to preach in India. I was with my friend, Bro. Dan Cash, a Christian businessman who flew me to India to preach and I was reading the great book, *The Foxes Book of Martyrs,* to help me pass the time during a thirty hour flight. As I read the pages of this book God started working in my heart. I read the stories of persecution that so many Christians endured for the cause of Christ. I read about how the Apostle Peter was crucified upside down on a cross at his own request. Because he felt that he was unworthy to die the same way Jesus died.

I read how Stephen was brutally pounded with stones until his crushed and bloody body gave up the ghost. I read how James, the brother of John, was put to death for preaching the Gospel. I read about Thomas who preached the Gospel to the Parthians, Medes, Persians, Carmanians, Hyrcanians, Bactrians, and Magians. He was killed for the cause of Christ in Calamina, India. Simon, (the little brother of Jude and James) was crucified in Egypt during the reign of the Roman emperor Trajan. Simon (the Apostle) preached in Mauritania, Africa and Britain was also crucified for the cause of Christ. Mark, who preached the Gospel in Egypt was put to death in a horrible way, death by burning. He was buried in a place called Bucolus. He was also put to death during the reign of the Roman emperor Trajan.

Bartholomew was beaten, then crucified and beheaded in Albinopolis, Armenia for the cause of Christ. Andrew, the brother of Peter, spent his life diligently preaching the Gospel. Aegeas, the Governor, asked permission of the Roman senate to force all Christianity to worship and make sacrifices to false Roman idols. Andrew went to Aegeas to compel him to give his life to Christ and to let him know that as a child of God he would resist his order. This made Aegeas very enraged and he ordered Andrew not to ever preach this "nonsense" again or else he would face a speedy crucifixion! At this, Andrew replied, "I would not have preached the honor and glory of the cross if I feared the death of the cross". Andrew was then condemned to die the horrible and painful death of crucifixion. This he endured for the love and glory of Christ.

Matthew preached the Gospel in Ethiopia and in Egypt. He was killed when King Hircanus had him knocked off by an assassins spear. Philip who was so brave and bold, spent most of his life preaching to rough, hardened, barbarous nations. He was in Hierapolis, Phrygia when he was stoned and then also crucified. He was then buried with his daughter. James, the little brother of Jesus, was murdered by a blood thirsty lynch mob in Jerusalem. He was buried where he fell. John the Baptist was put to death by King Herod who had him beheaded for his lovers daughter as a favor. He had John the Baptist's head delivered to her on a silver platter like some kind of macabre party gift. The Apostle Paul is said to have "lost his head for Jesus". He met his end on a butcher's block where he was beheaded for the cause of Christ. He was also stoned, beaten, and imprisoned.

All through history men and women have given the ultimate gift to God, their very life. So much was expected of them and they were willing to fulfill God's will to further the cause of Christianity.

In India, I met a dear pastor who became a dear friend. His name is Isaac. He is truly one of the most sincere men of God that I've ever known. While we were in India, he was our host. He set up all the great outdoor crusades that we had which yielded 1,450 souls saved in twelve days. He has a very painful health disorder that brings him much grief. I was astounded at how he just kept going and never complained. One night Bro. Dan, Bro. Isaac, and I were praying together when Bro. Isaac said something to God that broke my heart. He was asking God to help him make it in spite of his painful affliction. He said, "Lord, I'm in great pain but I know that I've never suffered as you've suffered." Right then, I felt a dagger in my heart. I thought about how Jesus suffered at his own free will to pay my debt, how he was beat, spat upon, punched, slapped, mocked, laughed at and betrayed. I thought about how He had His beard literally ripped out of his face by the roots. How He had a crown of thorns shoved onto his head. How He had a nine-inch rusty spike driven through both of his wrists and ankles. He was stripped of his clothes and hung naked in the blazing desert sun. He had a spear thrust into his side. Then, I thought of the things that I called persecution and it broke my heart. How I must sound to God when I complained about the opportunities to get to suffer for His name's sake, when Jesus paid so much more! I was filled with remorse and embarrassment.

What's the worst that most minister's kids endure for Jesus? Slight embarrassment, occasional ridicule, loss of certain social activities due to separation, some added pressure, none of this compares to the price paid by the disciples, early Christians, and Christians in foreign lands where Christians are despised and the sacrifice of our precious Saviour Jesus Christ.

Why some Christians are called upon to pay such a price for their Christianity and why it's God's will that some suffer for him in such horrible ways, and yet other Christians, (the average Christian) is called upon to give so little, is a mystery to me! I would like to think that I'd follow the example set forth by so many before me and lay down my life for the cause of Christ, if it were called upon. I do pray that I'll never have to be tested in this matter. It is my belief, however, that as a preacher's kid, we should be grateful at the small "persecutions" we endure and be proud that we have a chance to win a reward of faithfulness for Jesus' sake! When people treat us badly because of our faith and convictions then we can be proud that we've suffered in a small way for and with Jesus. In heaven none of us will want to tell of our pains when we are in the presence of the martyrs. It would be like a soldier complaining about a splinter in his finger to a soldier who has had his legs blown off. It just doesn't compare. I must say that in comparison any complaints of a P.K. really aren't that bad at all. Remember this the next time you wish to have a pity party and when you long to quit serving Jesus because of the "difficulties" you encounter.

> *"And they overcame him by the blood of the lamb, and by the word of their testimony; and they loved not their lives unto the death."*
>
> —Revelation 12:11

> *"Blessed are they which are persecuted for righteousness sake: for theirs is the kingdom of heaven. Blessed are ye, when man shall revile you, and persecute you, and shall say all manner of evil against you falsely; for my sake. Rejoice, and be exceeding glad: for great is your reward in heaven; for so persecuted they the prophets which were before you."*
>
> —Matthew 5:10-12

> *"Bless them which persecute you: bless, and curse not."*
>
> —Romans 12:14

> *"And labour, working with our own hands: being reviled, we bless; being persecuted, we suffer it: Being defamed, we*

intreat; we are made as the filth of the world, and are the offscouring of all things unto this day."

—I Corinthians 4:12 & 13

"Yea, and all that will live godly in Christ Jesus shall suffer persecution."

—II Timothy 3:12

6
Dangerous Attitudes

In this chapter I wish to deal with some fatal philosophies that are commonly developed among minister's kids. Those attitudes have been the noose that has choked the spirituality and joy out of the many P.K.'s who have harbored them. Let me try to point them out one by one. Let's see if you or someone you know has ever fought a round or two with them.

1. "The All or Nothing Syndrome"

"For a just man falleth seven times, and riseth up again: but the wicked shall fall into mischief."

—Proverbs 24:16

Many minister's kids have the subconscious attitude of all or nothing. By this, I mean, they think that if they can't be totally good then they will be totally bad. I've heard of P.K.'s who did a great job maintaining their purity for most of their premarried life. One night they succumbed to the always present temptation and gave their date a kiss. It could have stopped right there, but they felt that they had already messed up; and it's just a matter of time before somebody finds out and then they'll all think that I did more than just a kiss or two. So, I might as well just do it! Before they know it they've lost their purity, their testimony and their self- respect.

It seems with minister's kids that there is no middle ground. They are either extremely good kids who are active in the Lord's work, love their parents, love and obey them. They have a good testimony and over all, they do right. Then there are the kids who are extremely rebellious. They hate the church, Christian school, standards, church staff, rules, and at times it seems, they even hate their parents. They try everything! Drugs, alcohol, sex, the party lifestyle, and their testimony is one of shame. I see P.K.'s from both extremes. I rarely see kids who are in the middle. Kids who aren't professional Christian workers but do attend church regularly. Kids who have made mistakes but not huge ongoing mistakes. Kids who wish to not go into the ministry but have a high regard for it and those who do choose to go into it.

Most preacher's kids will be either gung ho, "all or nothing" kids who live to work for God and go about the world using their powers to do good . . . or they will be gung ho, "all or nothing" kids who live to buck the system, make their own decisions. They will leave behind a legacy of selfishness and a wake of hurt loved ones, tears, and regret. Their theme song is the song, "I did it my way". It seems that you could seek for a happy medium somewhere. You don't have to be the Apostle Paul but you don't have to be Judas Iscariot either. Do the best you can to be the best you can be. As a child of God, we realize that perfection is not possible in anyone and that as sinners, we are always in a fight to be righteous. The simple truth is, at times we'll lose a few battles in the war of righteousness but we must not ever drop out of the war.

2. "I just know that I'm missing out on something!"

"There is a way which seemeth right unto a man, but the end thereof are the ways of death."

—Proverbs 14:12

In Greek mythology, it is said that mystical creatures called mermaids lived in the ocean. They had the torso of a breathtakingly beautiful woman, and the bottom half, the fins and tail of a fish. They had such an intoxicating singing voice that sailors would jump out of the ship, and start swimming in the ocean towards the mystical voice until they were exhausted. The legend held that they would drown and be pulled to a watery grave while seeking pleasure and passions that, in reality, don't exist.

The attitude that is prevalent in many P.K.'s is that because of the life that is Christian, they are missing out on all the fun! They just know that they are missing the party and it drives them to a restless, frantic, search for the all night party that's going on somewhere, 24 hours a day, seven days a week. Many young Christians are enticed to the Devil's snare much the way the sailors of Greek mythology were driven to their demise by their thirst for an imagined pleasure.

I must admit that the Devil is so crafty at laying his vicious snare. I've seen so many entangled in his "come over here, it's so much better lie". There have been times that I even bought into it! I can still remember when I was a teenager it seemed that everything that looked fun was wrong and all the kids who were having a fun time with a life that was on the edge and full of adventure were "bad" kids. I remember that a part of me longed for a life with no dating standards, no curfews, no dress standards, no worries about what people thought about me!

It seemed that the boys who were wild and untamed, those "Rebels without a cause" types had to fight the girls off. They had their pick of whoever they wanted. Everybody wanted to be their friend. I would hear them tell of going to the mall, parties, cruising the town, and on dates with wild girls. While good guys, it seemed finished last. The envy would well up inside me and I'd hear those enticing voices singing in the deep driving me to my demise.

The reality is this, there is another life out there a life of bright lights and excitement. A life that at first drink, it's as sweet as honey and evokes feelings that will take you outside of yourself. Once you're in it, the sweet succulent taste turns to the putrid, bitter, taste of poison.

I've seen the end result of those who took a stroll on the dark side. I've watched as they've drowned in the ocean of regret, bad judgment, rebellion, and selfishness. The good girls who gave themselves to those wild childs had a great time until they got what they wanted and lost what they had. The wild ones were a lot of fun until it became time for commitment and they had to depend on them to pay the rent.

As a pastor, I met countless young women who told me they were raised in Christian homes but fled to the other life that they dreamed of. Now, they have a husband who won't come to church, is selfish and treats her like a guest. She'll cry because she thought that life was the answer to the "where's happiness" question but, instead, it's an illusion that stays just out of reach much like a mirage in the desolate desert.

Many will die in pursuit of the mythical other world. Many will try to return to the Christian life they left behind but it will never be the same. They'll bear the scars, cravings, and regret that will haunt them every dark night they spend alone.

The Devil has planted his picture of nirvana through the mediums of television, magazines, movies, music, and advocates strategically placed in the crowd that you associate with. There is a life that contains moments of fun, but wisdom tells us that the end result can only be tragedy. As a mature child of God, I now realize that there is indeed a life that I missed out on. When I see the results of those who lived it, I'm glad I missed out on it.

> "*Truly God is good to Israel, even to such as are of a clean heart. But as for me, my feet were almost gone my steps had well nigh slipped. For I was envious at the foolish, when I saw the prosperity of the wicked. For there are no bands in their death: but their strength is firm. They are not in trouble as other men; neither are they plagued like other men. Therefore pride compasseth them about as a chain; violence covereth as a garment. Their eyes stand out with fatness: they have more than heart could wish. They are corrupt, and speak wickedly concerning oppression: they speak loftily. They set their mouth against the heavens, and their tongue walketh through the earth. Therefore his people return hither: and waters of a full cup are wrung out to them.*

And they say, How doth God know: and is there knowledge in the most High? Behold, these are the ungodly, who prosper in the world; they increase in riches. Verily I have cleansed my heart in vain, and washed my hands in innocency. For all the day long have I been plagued, and chastened every morning. If I say, I will speak thus; behold, I should offend against the generation of thy children. When I thought to know this, it was too painful for me; Until I went into the sanctuary of God; then understood I their end. Surely, thou didst set them in slippery places; thou castedst them down into destruction. How are they brought into desolation, as in a moment! They are utterly consumed with terrors. As a dream when one awaketh; so, O Lord, when thou awakest, thou shalt despise their image. Thus my heart was grieved, and I was pricked in my reins. So foolish was I, and ignorant: I was as a beast before thee. Nevertheless I am continually with thee; thou hast holden me by my right hand. Thou shalt guide me with thy counsel, and afterward receive me to glory. Whom have I in heaven but thee? and there is none upon earth that I desire beside thee. My flesh and my heart faileth: but God is the strength of my heart, and my portion for ever. For, lo, they that are far from thee shall perish; thou hast destroyed all them that go a whoring from thee. But it is good for me to draw near to God: I have put my trust in the Lord God, that I may declare all thy works."

—Psalm 73

3. "If I hang around the wrong crowd I know I can pull them out of it."

We know this attitude is a practical impossibility. A law of physics is that it's always easier to pull down than it is to pull up! Dr. Jack Hyles said, "I don't hang around the wrong crowd because I'm afraid that I won't like them, I'm afraid that I will like them." The wrong crowd always portrays an image of freedom. They live by the, "I don't care what people think" motto. They all think they are so unique. It's funny, I talked to a young man once who had on baggy jeans and an oversized t-shirt, long sideburns, a shaved head, and he had a scraggly goatee with tattoos and several painful looking body piercings. He said that he got them to show the world that he was different and unique. I then looked around me at all the teens in the mall that we were both standing in. I didn't see a single one in there with a short, neat haircut, clean shaved face, a shirt and jeans that fit and a body with no holes punched into it. I did see however a small army of teens who looked just like him, all with the same delusion that they were different. They looked boringly all the same to me. I certainly didn't see any with the guts to be Christians and look like it. The truth is they do care what people think and their desperate attempt to look like their friends and heroes proves it.

The wrong crowd will make you think they are loyal to the end and would never, "rat you out" at any cost. Eight years of being a youth pastor has forever proven that to be a lie to me. Those kids will sell you out so quick it'll make your head spin! I've seen those loyal friends to the end, turn tail and run every time it came to saving their own necks!

I've seen many good kids become bad with the wrong crowd. I've never seen one bad crowd become good through a good kid infiltrating it. They will make you think, that because they don't tell on you or pass judgment on you, because they assist you in your plans of deceit and pretend to still respect and love you, that they are better friends than the ones who try to play the role of conscience and tell you that you are wrong. The Bible says . . .

> *"Faithful are the wounds of a friend; but the kisses of an enemy are deceitful".*
>
> —Proverbs 27:6

The truth is it takes a lot of love to risk losing a friendship to help a friend. The wrong crowd never demonstrates true love in their willingness to help you hurt yourself. Any friend who will encourage you to sneak around, lie, disobey, smoke, drink, and do drugs is an advocate of the Devil and enemy of God. There's a saying that says, "I fear the Greeks even when they come bearing gifts." This is said as a result of the legend of the Trojan horse. The story of the war between Troy and Greece. Greece presented a huge wooden horse as a peace offering to Troy. The Trojan warriors pulled the horse into the walls of the mighty fortress that had been impenetrable. That night a small hatch opened up and a small group of soldiers climbed out and unlocked the gate. The Greek army spilled in and overtook the city. For many P.K.'s the end will start when they let some "Greek" bearing gifts of friendship into the walls of their life and that friend will unlock the gates for the forces of Satan to overtake them. When you are with the wrong crowd you are the wrong crowd. When they fall, they will take you down with them!

> *"Blessed is the man that walketh not in the counsel of the ungodly, nor standeth in the way of sinners, nor sitteth in the seat of the scornful. But his delight is in the law of the Lord, and in his law doth he meditate day and night. And he shall be like a tree planted by the rivers of water, that bringeth forth his fruit in his season; his leaf also shall not wither; and whatsoever he doeth shall prosper. The ungodly are not so: but are like the chaff which the wind driveth away. Therefore the ungodly shall not stand in the judgment, nor sinners in the congregation of the righteous. For the Lord knoweth the way of the righteous: but the way of the ungodly shall perish."*
>
> —Psalm 1

> *"My son, if sinners entice thee, consent thou not. If they say, Come with us, let us lay wait for blood, let us lurk privily for the innocent without cause: Let us swallow them up alive as the grave; and whole, as those that go down into the pit: We shall find all precious substance, we shall fill our houses with spoil; Cast in thy lot among us; let us all have one purse: My son, walk not thou in the way with them; refrain thy foot from their path: For their feet run to evil, and make haste to shed blood. Surely in vain the net is spread in the sightof any bird. And they lay wait for their own blood; they lurk privily for their own lives."*
>
> —Proverbs 1:10-18

"Enter not into the path of the wicked, and go not in the way of evil men. Avoid it, pass not by it, turn from it, and pass away. For they sleep not except they have done mischief; and their sleep is taken away, unless they cause some to fall. For they eat the bread of wickedness, and drink the wine of violence. But the path of the just is as the shining light, that shineth more and more unto the perfect day.The way of the wicked is as darkness: they know not at what they stumble. My son, attend to my words; incline thine ear unto my sayings."

—Psalms 4:14-20

4. My Dad is a Nobody.

I think the politics of the ministry is one of the hardest aspects of the ministry. It seems that the modern day view of success is so different from the views set forth in the word of God. Many have unsuspectingly bought into it.

The view of a successful pastor today is a pastor who has a mega church with 500 to 3,000 or more members. He must have a Christian school, a college, a large staff, the letters Ph.D. behind his name and he must be preaching all over America.

Some groups will look at how many baptisms he's had, others will judge him by how fast his church has grown. There are lists of churches who are deemed as successful by the powers that be. Every pastor hopes to pastor a mega church with multi-faceted ministries and a huge breathtaking facility. This won't , however, be the story for most men of God.

Most men of God go unnoticed, unappreciated, and unknown. They quietly go about the Lord's work being a help where he can. He'll go to a facility that is woefully inadequate. He'll work alone with no secretary or staff to meet with and plan with. He'll study hard for hours to preach to the same 50 - 100 people every Sunday. He'll go home discouraged at his life of insignificance. He'll look at his reflection in the mirror and he'll feel a consolation come into his heavy, broken heart and say, "At least, I've been faithful." That night he'll go to bed and dream of that glorious day when he preaches to a packed church with altars full and people saying, "Pastor, that was the greatest sermon I've ever heard!" He'll smile in his blissful slumber only to wake up on Monday morning to the reality. He pastors a small church and he is a small man of God.

I had more than one P.K. ask me a question with anticipation in their voice and hope in their eyes. Have you ever heard of my dad? I've seen the crushed look as they've heard the answer, "No" return to their anxious ears. Many times I've acted as though the name was familiar just because I've been on the receiving end of that scenario. It's a kickback to our childhood days when we earnestly believed that Daddy could beat up Superman and solve every problem that would ever arise. We'd like to think of our dads as big important men who are well known and respected. Somehow this makes the P.K. feel bigger and a little more important.

There are some things we must all recognize. One, there are no small jobs in God's work. Not all pastors are going to be able to pastor large well-known churches. As a P.K. who has been on both ends of the ruler, I can say that it takes a lot of variables to build a mega church. It's not God's will that all men pastor huge churches and have a ministry that is renown. A man of God is called to be faithful not famous. There are churches in big towns and someone's got to pastor there.

There are also churches that are in small rural areas that can never run thousands or even hundreds. Some body has got to be willing to be a pastor to those churches, to love and guide those people. Your dad may be one of the men who can take a church with special needs and carefully shepherd those people.

Two, God has his own view of success and his own method of rewarding his men and servants. I do believe that a lot of the "Big Guns" that we see preaching everywhere are receiving a lot of their reward now! Their goal many times is not to win souls as much as to win recognition, to be the leader, to have the biggest church. There is nothing wrong in having a huge church but there is also nothing wrong in having a small but strong, Bible preaching, and growing church. My papaw pastored several churches over a forty year period. He never pastored a huge church but he's lead thousands of souls to Christ. He's seen several of his little boys grow up to pastor churches and lead even more souls to Christ. He started three churches which today bear no memory of him, there's not even a plaque in the lobby stating him as the founder. But God knows and it didn't go unnoticed and one day God will reward him accordingly.

Three, a lot of those men have paid a huge price for their celebrity. They have no spare time. They are gone all the time. They miss birthdays and anniversaries. They spend a lot of time feeling lonely and despite their success they often feel inadequate. Each year they feel the pressure to beat the last year. When you're known for being the pastor of a big church, you better hope your church stays big! For many of these men, their whole identity is in the size of their ministry. Many of them have lost their families to be successful and many of them have spent thirty years in a blink, as they went through life always looking to the future and never able to enjoy the present.

Four, to you, the greatest preacher in the world should be your daddy! As I grew up I got to hear all the greats often. They come to our church to preach revivals and conferences. Dr. Hyles, Dr. Lee Roberson, Dr. Jim Vinyard, Dr. Dennis Corle, Dr. Johnny Pope, Dr. Carl Hatch, Dr. Jim Brown, Dr.B.R.Laken, Dr. Mickey Carter, and the list goes on and on. My brothers, sisters, and I had a little tradition with our dad. We'd say, "That preacher was good but not near as good as you, Daddy!" He'd smile from ear to ear as he'd reach to kiss us on the cheek. Last month I was with my dad. He preached at a conference with several "Big Name" preachers.

I'm twenty-nine years old but I said, "Dad those guys preached great sermons but none were better than you were!" He smiled and kissed his son on the cheek.

To this day I'd rather hear my dad preach more than any other pulpiteer that's out there. To me, he is the greatest preacher and church builder in the world! Sure, he doesn't pastor the biggest church in the world but I know he could if God gave it to him. It's not been God's will for him. I spoke to a young P.K. the other day and I asked him who the greatest preacher was. He didn't bat an eye as he said, "My daddy". I just looked at him and smiled because I knew the truth. The greatest preacher is my daddy!

Don't ever think less of your daddy than the fact that he is a man of God and a soldier of the cross. He is one who does the most important work in the whole world, God's work. And God chose him personally to do it.

5. No one else believes what we believe.

Elisha got to thinking this way when he said, "I'm the only one who serves you, God". God had to reveal that there were thousands who had not bent their knee to false gods! I remember many times thinking that there are no other Christians who are as strict as we are! They're all liberals, and weirdoes or snobs.

I now know that all over America there are P.K.'s who are trying to live right and serve God. There are preachers who still preach the old message from the old Book. There are families by the thousands who still have standards and convictions. Don't buy into this "pity party" that you are the only one who still loves, obeys, and serves the King! Just go to some youth rallies and pastor's conferences and you'll see what I'm saying. At the time of this writing I am the director of the Future Fundamentalists of Florida organization. A group that God lead me to start with the purpose of encouraging todays youth. Every third Friday of the month we have a rally. There have been hundreds of teens at every one of these rallies. God's work is still alive in the hearts of others. Don't feel like you are the last of an extinct breed.

6. I need to prove I'm as cool as everybody else!

This attitude is dangerous because it can turn a brilliant young P.K. into a fool! This philosophy goes hand in hand with peer pressure. In order to prove that you are cool, hip, with it and fun, you'll do things that you know are wrong to prove you're just as normal as them. I've heard of kids cursing, drinking, doing drugs, even engaging in sexual activity, just to show others they are cool.

They don't want people to say that they are geeks, or "holy Joe" types. A weird thing about being a P.K. is that often they are targeted as trophies by the wrong crowd. Much like a hunter who looks for a trophy buck or moose. I've seen boys who were no good and of questionable character put their sights on the pastor's daughter just to see if he can get her. Once he gets her and spoils her virginity, reputation, testimony and parental trust, he's through with her! Many times it's this attitude that makes it possible for him to make the kill! Many times, what you perceive to be dislike from the others because you are a strong Christian is actually envy, respect or intimidation. Don't let the desire for earthly acceptance inspire you to do evil and therefore lose heavenly acceptance. The world may act like they like you but they don't respect you. Don't become a trophy for them. Make them come up to your level and don't stoop to theirs!

7. I feel that I cannot win either way I go.

As a P.K. there were times when I wondered if people would have liked me better if I had gone into the world, messed up my life, lived in rebellion and kept everybody on their knees in prayer for me. I could've then returned a heralded prodigal son who was lost but is now found! A boy who was lost in the winds of confusion while trying to find himself. I wondered if it would have made me even more down to earth, more likable and more easy to identify with. It would have made me less of an example but more of a comrade to the scores of mediocre Christians who could say "Rusty's one of us".

As a young preacher, I've noticed that just about every big name preacher was an ex-something. They now use their testimony to help others. It's a great thing when you hear that God has wonderfully changed someone's life. It's great to see a person who has seen themselves for how they really are and drop to their knees for God to save and restore them. But sometimes, it's this very sinful, rebellious and selfish life that they've led that makes them famous and loved later! I've even heard youth pastors say that they believe that it's good that they sowed their wild oats, so that they could better understand the plight of the wandering lambs in their group. I wish to say that I disagree whole heartedly with this whole attitude! When one tries to sell this philosophy they display a severe wisdom deficiency. No where in the Bible do we see where the prodigal son became better or more useful because he went into sin. He was restored and forgiven but we don't read that he received a second inheritance to replace the one he so recklessly squandered. We don't see that God commended him for his ability to see that he was foolish for eating pig slop when he could go home and at least eat better as a servant in his father's home. He did however have a brother who stayed home and didn't pursue rebellion. The Bible says that the faithful son felt just as I did many times. He felt that everybody loved the prodigal son more. He felt that because he stayed home and did right he was taken for granted. No party was ever given in his honor, and no fatted calf was ever cooked for him! He felt that he would have been noticed and appreciated more if he had followed his brother into the land of waste.

Have you ever looked around you and felt this way? I remember when I was a teenager in a Christian school. There was another student in my class who was a very hard case. He was likable and very good looking. He came from a very influential family in our church. He was the kind of guy who every girl noticed and desired. He was a typical teenager, he'd do what was best for him first and if you were in the way, then that's just too bad. He was used to getting what he wanted. He was a smooth operator who'd do just enough good things to keep the teachers and staff thinking there was hope for him and they all felt they were the key to his success. If they'd just give him some extra attention, praise, and personal one on one training then he'd make it. Meanwhile, I and my friends felt jealous of the attention he got. He was getting to go with the youth director on trips and the principal would get him out of class and allow him to go running around with him. Even one basketball coach, who was an unusually hard man, gave him favors because he was an excellent athlete. He did several things that the coach would bench or even suspend us for and all he got was extra laps or a lecture which would then be followed up with praise to show him that he was still loved! He did things such as cut class, get into fights, curse at school, skip church, not go soul winning, (which was required to be a basketball player in our school). He even engaged another boy in a contest to see how many girls in our Christian school he could get carnal knowledge of! My own girlfriend became my ex-girlfriend when it became known that she was a pawn in his little game. I and my friends went to soul winning, church, youth activities and school. We tried to avoid trouble, be an example and please the staff. It seemed that the more we did, the more they expected and the harder it seemed to please them. The less he did, the less they expected and the more they'd praise him.

For example, he would do something good, something that the rest of us did everyday but when we'd do it, it would go unnoticed, when he'd do it, they'd talk about it for days! He'd be used as an example, they'd tell about it in the staff meetings, chapel and testimony services.

I know that I and my friends all fell into faulty reasoning that he had it made, the best of both worlds. He had his cake and was going to eat it too. However, as they say, "It all comes out in the wash". Today that young man is an example of a life that had so much invested but gave so little in return. He has been in and out of several dry-out centers to help him with his drug and alcohol addictions. He's been married twice and is now divorced. He's wrecked several cars including a corvette that he custom ordered for his sixteenth birthday. He has contracted a venereal disease and his once handsome face is now scarred by years of sin. My friends and I are now grown up. My best friends are doing great! They're married and raising a family. They also have great jobs. Phil Graham and Jensen Payte who were my best friends both live a life that is pleasing to God and they are both successful. You see, it's character that always makes a person, not opportunity, silver spoons, attention or charm! The boy who stayed home ended up inheriting all that his father had! For the rest of his life he had it good while his prodigal brother thought about what could have been his if he had been wise. A life of sin leaves permanent scars!

Recently, a preacher friend of mine got involved with another woman and lost his whole family. I remember him telling me once, "Rusty, you're so lucky! You had a godly upbringing with rules and strict parents, Christian schooling and morals." He said, "I got saved when I was 23. I had done drugs and alcohol. I lived a very promiscuous lifestyle. Now, those things haunt me!" He said, "I have a hard time in not desiring strange flesh, pornography and alcohol. Even though I've tried to change, those demons come to call when I'm alone." It was no surprise to any of us when we heard that he'd engaged in adultery with a teenage girl in his church. He's lost his wife, ministry and testimony. You understand, he was trained by the world and the world owned him. Even though he tried to escape, the guardians would track him down and drag him right back in. You are so much better off to not have a bunch of skeletons in your closet as a result of being envious of the wicked! In the long run, good guys at least finish the race.

"It is not wealth, nor ancestry, but honorable conduct and noble disposition that make man great."

—Ovid

7

Why Do So Many P.K.'s Go Bad?

(and how to prevent becoming a statistic)

We all know that rebellion among minister's kids is rampant. It's a sad but true reality that is seen among our special fraternity. In writing this book, I've sat across the table of many men of God. I've watched as their eyes swell up with tears and heard their usually strong, sure voices turn wavy and weak. As their head turns to the ground they say, "I don't know where it all went wrong". "I try to think back and find things I would have done differently, but I can find nothing." Many of them go on to tell of how their child's earliest memories were of their mom and me praying in their ear, having a family altar, taking them to the nursery, then to Sunday school and children's church, vacation Bible school, church camp, and then later, the teen group and youth rallies. They say to me, "I spent a fortune on Christian Education". They say, "We home schooled our children to keep them away from the wrong crowd". We did everything we were taught to do to "train up a child in the way he should go". And yet our child is living in horrible, wicked, shameful sin. My child is breaking my heart! How could this happen? All I could do was just sit there and shake my head in heavy somber empathy.

I've talked to P.K.'s who are: single teen-age moms, drug addicts, alcoholics, living in adultery, serving sentences in the penitentiary, married to lost and godless mates, divorced multiple headed towards a sad but inevitable collision with the wrath of the Almighty God.

I've looked into their cold, dark eyes and seen the fires of rage, bitterness, depression, hatred, selfishness, insecurity, confusion, disorientation, denial and pure evil. I've wondered what the end will be and when. Most of all I've wondered, why? How could they be this way? How could they resent this special calling in their life? Why is the fraternity of P.K. hood turning out such a band of losers?

I'm sure there are a host of reasons why P.K.'s turn to the dark side. Inconsistencies in the home, hypocrisy, parents who don't spend time with their child, some men of God are great pastors but horrible dads as Eli was. These may be some of the reasons. Maybe it was wrong friends, TV, magazines, poor school options, bad home life, the politics of church life. I don't know. Any of these variables could play a part in destroying a life.

I do know this, in most cases, it wasn't bad parenting, as much as it was bad judgment on the part of the child. I know for a fact that in many Christian homes that have experienced the blinding blow of a child who follows the will of Satan, the parents did all they could humanly do, to be good, godly, loving and supportive parents!

There's a Flaw in our Reasoning . . .

We like to believe that the apple never falls far from the tree. That a bad child is always a result of bad parenting. This is incorrect! I've heard it taught that everything rises and falls on leadership. I believe that leadership is very important but I don't know that good leadership is always going to guarantee success. Many times, we've seen examples of great leaders who felt the sting of defeat and the despair of mediocrity because they had bad followers. Adam and Eve are examples of this fact! They had a relationship with God that was unparalleled. God walked with them in the Garden of Eden. He shared intimacy and close fellowship with His ultimate creation. He was their leader. We all know the tragic ending to the story. Adam and Eve failed. It wasn't that they were the victims of poor leadership! They were victims of their own poor followship. In the Bible every great leader started out a great follower and all of them followed God. From Moses to David, from David to Elisha, from Elisha to Peter, from Peter to Judas Iscariot and from Judas Iscariot to today, men have been made or broke on their ability to follow God at all costs. Many churches have been destroyed even though they had pastors who are strong leaders. The problem was they had deacons, assistant pastors or members who were weak followers. Most kids who are raised in godly homes and still go bad, will go bad because of their inability to follow God!

What's the Answer?

It's always been taught that to raise a child to serve the Lord and be holy, you need "The Big Three Elements" in their life. The three elements being: one, a godly home; two, a strong, separated church; three, a godly education system.

I've seen parents try unsuccessfully to raise God fearing kids by one out of the three, or two out of the three elements. I have a Christian school in my church. I'm amazed at the number of parents who have come to me with problem children. They have had their kids in every Christian school in the county but their kids still can't seem to walk on the straight and narrow path. I'll ask them where they go to church and I'm never shocked when they reply that they don't go to church regularly. They expect Christian school to be the "cure all" for years of spiritual neglect, inconsistency, hypocrisy and bad judgment. The fact is, a Christian home without a strong, Bible teaching church is lacking a major element of success.

A Christian school student without a godly home and consistent church attendance is also missing major elements of success. The weird thing is, I've seen kids whose parents were lost and godless, kids who go to the cesspool of public schools and not have the benefit of a strong church for most of their childhood turn out to be some of the greatest, strongest Christians that I've ever had the privilege to meet. Now let's get real heavy.

I've seen kids who had it all, the Christian home, strong church, and Christian education turn out to be some of the most horrible waste of DNA in the world! The truth is, most preachers hate preaching in Christian school chapels! I've been to funerals that had more enthusiasm than some of the Christian school chapels I've preached in! What's the difference? How can two children be raised in the same Christian home, one follow God, and the other Satan? I want to introduce to you a fourth element that has been largely overlooked. Yet, this fourth element is the most crucial of all the elements of raising a Christian child.The fourth element is a personal love for God!

A child in a Christian home will be imposed to go to church, attend the family altar, read the Bible, abide by the rules of separation and go to a private Christian school. In my home, I had no choice in these matters! I was expected to be at the family altar times. It didn't matter if I was playing basketball or in the middle of the highest scoring game of Pacman ever, when Dad called us kids to come to the living room for devotions, we came! I was expected to go soul winning, read my Bible, get good grades, act right and be an example. I remember that the "Wonderful World of Disney" would come on every Sunday night at 5:30. I had to leave right in the middle of it every time to get to church by 6:30. I saw the first 30 minutes of *Old Yeller* several times and I was 20 years old before I ever saw the ending to it! I cried like a baby when I saw that the grand old dog had to be shot by the boy! I remember being mad more than once because I had to leave my good fun to go to a long, boring church service.

I was thirteen years old when I went to Triple "S" Christian Ranch in Rose Bud, Arkansas where Evangelist John Bishop ran a church camp. I had gone to camp every year since I was eight years old. Most of the time I had fun but I didn't get too much out of the preaching. But that year something happened to me that forever changed me. I actually listened to the sermon. The preacher said only one out of a hundred of you will make it. Most of you will fall by the wayside and ruin your life because everything you do for God is only because you have to do it and not because you actually love God. It hit me like a hammer! I knew he was right. Up until then, everything I'd been doing was because it was imposed upon me! I wanted to change, to no longer do it because I had to, but because I loved God!

I was dazed with the powerful blow of conviction and I went to the altar and committed to God that if only one out of a hundred will make it, then I want to be the one out of this hundred to still be serving you, even when mom and dad can no longer make me do it!

Through the years I've seen most of the other 99 go astray. But, somehow, I'm still here. I can't explain it. I look at my sister Christy, she's married to a pastor who is a godly man. She has always had a deep love for Jesus that I respected. My younger brother Sam, who pastors a church, I know he loves the Lord and seeks to please him and do his bidding.

My other younger brother Danny is a professor of History and is a great man of God who still gets tears in his eyes when he preaches about how God saved him. My lovely wife who is the single greatest gift that God has given me (next to salvation) is a pastor's daughter who serves God wholeheartedly with her life. All those people have one element in common. They have a personal love for their Lord and Saviour, and that alone is why they strive to be righteous, do the work of the Lord, and stay on the path, just following the Lord where he leads!

You see, love for God is the one element that is missing in the lives of many Christian young people, certainly many P.K.'s! They look at love for God as a burden and not a blessing. It is impossible to rebel against the fourth element because it can never be imposed upon you! No one can make you love anyone in your heart. You must decide yourself! The choice is purely yours in the end to follow and love the one who loved you enough to die for you or love yourself and follow the one who is dying to destroy you.

I remember one of my earliest childhood memories is of my mom placing me on the bed and teaching me the verse from the

Bible that said, "Thou shalt love the Lord thy God with all thy heart and with all thy soul, and with all thy might." I know my parents put me in an environment that was conducive to falling in love with God. Yet, the choice was totally mine. I don't know why personal love for God is in the heart of some but not in most. I don't even know how to tell a parent a way to guarantee it. Some wars can only be fought on your knees. This may be one of them. All I can say is this, from the age of thirteen on, I've discovered the joy of having a friend in my Saviour, Jesus Christ. Maybe you know Jesus but you've never developed a love for Him. I can't help but think of Judas. He was a disciple who saw Jesus, heard Jesus teach, traveled with Jesus and was trusted by Jesus. He saw the miracles and the love of Christ. Yet, he died lost. Why? Because he never developed a love for Christ in his own heart. There was a man who died one time who was known for being a very good man. He was charitable and moral. Although strangely, he didn't go to church, and confessed that he'd never asked Jesus to save him. At his funeral, the preacher said, "He missed heaven by 18 inches". The people looked at the preacher with looks of bewilderment. Then he explained 18 inches is the length from his brain to his heart. You see, even though the man had a head knowledge of God his heart was a cold, black, empty vessel. He never let his heart be filled with love for the King. This eulogy sadly awaits many of the P.K.'s of today. I hope that you are more than that! Seek to love God personally today and you just might make it through your life behind the walls of glass!

"Love for God is displayed when the smile of God is your greatest delight and His frown is your greatest dread."

—Dr. Glenn Riggs

8

Don't Just Take My Word For It!

Christy Riggs
Apopka Baptist Temple, Apopka, Florida

Hello, my name is Christy Riggs. I was born on June 24, 1977 in Bessemer, Alabama. And when I was two years old both of my parents accepted Christ as their personal Saviour, and shortly after that my dad surrendered his life to serve the Lord full time as a preacher.

When I was six years old my parents, my two younger brothers and myself all headed to Hammond, Indiana where my dad attended and graduated from Hyles Anderson College. During this time my younger sister was born.

After my dad graduated he accepted a position in Tavares, Florida as an assistant pastor and principal of a Christian school. Then my dad pastored Harvest Baptist in Florida, then Faithway Baptist in Illinois and from there back to Florida to where he is now pastoring Lighthouse Baptist Church in Eustis, Florida. As you can see we moved around quite a bit. I considered this to be one of the harder things in our ministry, because it meant at times moving to a different school or being home schooled, and it meant making new friends all over again.

Another thing hard about being a P.K. was you are always being watched. Some people can not wait to find dirt on the pastor's family, to catch us doing any little thing wrong just so that they could blow it out of proportion. They would forget that we are only human just as they are. Even though this was hard to deal with at times, I believe that it was one of the things that helped bring me out of a rebellious stage that I went through when I was a teenager. I did not want to ruin my family name.

Despite the things that were difficult in my life as a P.K., I am very thankful that I was raised in a preacher's home. I would not have had it any other way. It is something that we should be proud of instead of trying to hide it from people.

I learned to be a soul winner by example of my parents whom I consider to be two of the greatest soul winners I have ever known. I learned to have a desire to serve the Lord by the training I had in the years of growing up.

Now, I am married to a preacher, my husband, Russell Riggs. I never had any intention of marrying a preacher but God had different plans for my life. So being raised in a pastor's home helped prepare me a little more for my life as an adult.

I have great respect for my parents, Michael and Jolyn Watkins, my dad who is a wonderful pastor and my mom, a wonderful pastor's wife. They are my heroes, and I am thankful for how they raised me, and for teaching me to love the Lord. And I have a great respect for my husband. He is a wonderful pastor and husband. And I hope that our children will love the ministry as we do.

Jesse Barker

Forrest Baptist Church, Apopka, Florida

Hi. My name is Jesse Barker. I was born on January 19, 1988 at Florida Hospital in Orlando. I have a sister, Erika. Erika is eight years old. She goes to Lovell Elementary.

My family goes to Forrest Avenue Baptist Church in Apopka, Florida. My grandfather is our pastor. My dad is assistant pastor. He preaches when my grandfather is away.

I like being a Preacher's Kid. I get to visit other churches. My sister and I were saved at Forrest Avenue Baptist Church. Our grandfather baptized us. He also baptized my dad and mommy.

My Uncle Joe is a missionary to Paraguay. My Uncle Ted is a missionary to Albania and works in Kosovo. My Aunt Amy and her husband, Glenn, is a missionary to Russia.

My grandfather was saved at nine years old. My dad was saved when he was six years old. My grandfather started Glendale Baptist Church in Maudlin, South Carolina. I like being a Preacher's Kid.

Joshua Watkins
Lighthouse Baptist Church, Eustis, Florida

Hi. My name is Joshua Watkins. My dad is the pastor of Lighthouse Baptist Church.

I was born January 30, 1983 in Leesburg, Florida. I was seven months old when my parents and three kids, counting me, left for Hammond, Indiana to go to Hyles-Anderson College. My little sister was born during this time. We were there until 1990 when we moved back to Florida.

Since then my dad has been a principal, an assistant pastor, and is now pastor. My pastor, which is my dad, and my hero, are currently at Lighthouse Baptist Church. God is working miraculously in Lighthouse Baptist Church, a beautiful facility.

Because of his experience during this time, I believe my dad is a better man, a better father, and a better pastor. Being a P.K. has it's ups and downs. I've seen prayers answered and fulfilled. I'm glad I grew up in a godly family. Being a P.K., you always have a church family and your own family are always there to protect and love you, and to make sure you stay right with God. They always encourage you to do the right thing. My family and I are blessed in many ways because of being faithful to God. There are many good things about being a Preacher's Kid. But there is always a downfall. When there is no youth group, there is no friends. That is just one of the few downfalls. I try not to look at things I don't like about it. I try to look at the things that I do like. I'm praying for what God shall do with my life when I graduate in a year. This is my life verse and goal: Romans 12:1, 2 - I beseech you therefore, brethren, by the mercies of God, that ye present your bodies a living sacrifice, holy, acceptable unto God, which is your reasonable service. And be not conformed to this world but be ye transformed by the renewing of your mind, that ye may prove what is that good, and acceptable, and perfect, will of God.

Steven Carter

Landmark Baptist Church, Haines City, Florida

My name is Steven Carter and I am the son of Dr. Mickey Carter, Pastor of the Landmark Baptist Church in Haines City, Florida. My father has been pastoring in Haines City for over 28 years. I have been around for 25 of them. The Lord has blessed me with a beautiful wife of 4 years, Paula, and a fifteen month old, wonderful baby girl named Shay! I have been serving on church staff for about four and a half years. I'm currently the director of the Young Married Department (Sweetheart Couples Class) and enrolled part time in the Masters program at Landmark Baptist College. Lord willing I will be graduating next year with my Masters in Pastoral Theology along with my Bachelors in Christian Administration.

The Bible says in Luke 12:48 b, "For unto whomsoever much is given, of him shall much be required." This verse states a very familiar truth. A truth that would have to apply to a Preacher's Kid as much as anyone that comes to mind. Recently, a young man that grew up in the home of an alcoholic asked me if I felt like I missed out or was deprived of certain things while growing up in a preacher's home. He mentioned that he had talked to a few preacher's kids before and that was the impression that he received. I quickly answered and told him that I did not believe that I missed out on anything, except taking full advantage of the opportunity God has given me.

The Bible says in James 4:17, "Therefore to him that knoweth to do good, and doeth it not, to him it is a sin." The life of a preacher's son does come with many peaks and valleys, but the experience is something very special that I would not trade for anything. It seems that the unique pressures of being a preacher's kid does drive some folks away from the ministry, but there are many children who have turned out right and are now heavily involved in the ministry. When you are able to witness first hand the watchful care of the Lord as he guides and protects your parents and always provides in due time no matter how big the need. It is difficult to turn away from your own calling of the Lord.

I thank the Lord for God's calling on my life. Looking back at my upbringing, I do have some regrets when I think of how long I waited to fully surrender my life to the Lord. It seems as though you can become complacent, taking for granted the ministry that you have been raised in relying on your father to shoulder the load. My father is my Pastor, my boss, my friend, and my hero. I thank the Lord each day for the opportunity to serve with him in the work God has entrusted him with.

Bethany Watkins

Lighthouse Baptist Church, Eustis, Florida

Hi. I am Bethany Watkins. My father is Michael Watkins. He is now the pastor at Lighthouse Baptist Church. I was born in Merillville, Indiana where my dad was going to Bible college at Hyles-Anderson College. I was born on July 9, 1985. I am the fourth child born in our family. My dad was in college from 1983 to 1990. After college, we went to Florida, where the rest of the family was mainly from, to Liberty Baptist Church and school in Tavares, Florida. Where my family was going before Bible college. Dad became the principal of the school and the assistant pastor of the church for a year.

Then things started happening that my dad disagreed with, so he felt it was time to move on. So he started Harvest Baptist Church. We began in our house with about ten people. A few weeks later the church rented a little store front. The church grew to be a good church. But God called him on, so he resigned the church. He helped a few other churches to grow. Then we went to Illinois to a church up there. It was hard leaving all my family and friends living in Florida. But it was what God wanted for us. So my dad pastored at Faithway Baptist Church. I met new people and grew to love them, but they did not want to serve God by going soul winning and by building the church.

So we came back to Florida where my dad co-pastored at Lighthouse Baptist Church. The pastor was in bad health when he retired. My dad became pastor and this is where we have been for the last three years, serving the people with us and God faithfully. We have had ups and downs, lost and gained people, friends have gone that you had to let go. It's hard sometimes to do the things you should not do while watching the world do all the fun things, you are at church serving and soul winning, not like the world. But in the long run, we will be better off. A preacher's kid is the best thing because you are very blessed by God.

The God of Our Fathers

Rev. Joel D. Tillis, *Assoc. Pastor*

Open Door Baptist Church

In the sovereign plan of our Lord, it has been my lot and blessing to be the son of a Gospel Preacher. As in most things, there is the sweet of this life and there is the bitter. I have seen countless multitudes come to know Christ, but I have seen the most loyal of followers turn to try to destroy my father. I have seen ministries swell with the power and the blessing of God, but I have also seen churches split through carnality and blind anger. Being the son of a Preacher, I have had the privilege of standing at the very feet of Fundamentalism's foremost Preachers. And yet, I have seen many fall disgracefully breaking the hearts of thousands. Truly, as a "preacher's kid", there is a danger of bitterness and hurt, but I believe that there is a greater and more subtle danger that ravages the lives of untold myriads of preacher's kids. Simply put, it is the fact of not knowing the God that they are being taught to serve.

In the great majority of cases, the root of the problem is not our relationship with our dad, or lack thereof, nor is it the bitterness that arises over the hypocrisies within the church. The root is, preacher's kids often have the form of godliness, but have denied the power thereof. From the first time we are enrolled in

Sunday school, we are taught and weaned in the service of the ministry. We know the right words, say the right things, carry the right Bible, pray the right way, obtain the right amount of professions of faith at visitation, dress the right way, and yet, for all of our activity, we know very little of the God we are serving. Few and far between are those children of the ministry who go on to walk in the power and fullness of the Holy Spirit. Why, one may ask? Because of two basic reasons. First of all, in many cases, the spirituality of the preacher's kid is simply "assumed" due to their level of involvement and activity in the ministry. However the landscape strewn with the wasted lives of preacher's kids should emphatically tell us that activity does not, nor cannot, substitute for spirituality. Secondly, many times there is a tendency to live off of the Pastor's Christianity. The messages and the power of their fathers seems often to take the place of a personal walk with the Lord. These two fundamental problems leave the preacher's kid an open prey to the wiles of the devil. All he must do is burn them out on their work, or show the frailty of their father's Christianity, and they have nothing else to stand on. Preacher's kids must be taught more than any one, that the secret is not in effort and activity, but in the power and personal relationship of the sacred Spirit. This problem is seen clearly in the Bible. Absalom was a powerful leader who had learned well how to run his father's ministry. He knew all the workings of leadership and service, yet he did not know the God of his father David. Solomon, however, was called young and tender by his father. David was concerned that he would not be a strong enough leader. However, Solomon was a great leader, not because of his ability, but because he had followed on to know the God of his father.

Preacher's kids cannot settle to hear their fathers speak about a God they've never known. They must follow on to know the Lord for themselves. To ignore this is to ignore the very root of what is at stake. Relationships can be healed and mended, love can be nurtured and grown, bitterness can be soothed in the washing of time, but nothing can take the place for the desperate need of walking in the Spirit. As preacher's kids we must understand, that our ministry, as all Christians, is first to ourselves. Walk in the Spirit and the power thereof, and all other things will find their proper place. This very thought has been my source of strength and stability. It is a battle we are in. Be strong therefore in the power of the Lord.

9

Raising A Minister's Kid

On March 11, 2000 an amazing thing happened to me. An event that has forever changed the way I view my life, the way I live my life, and the very purpose of my existence. On March 11, 2000 my beautiful wife gave birth to my gorgeous daughter Savannah Renee Riggs. I stood in absolute amazement as she was brought forth kicking and screaming, into the madness we call life.

I'll never forget the moment the doctor handed her to me the first time, she was just minutes old. I held her tiny body in my hands, I felt her chest as her little heart pounded and her bold blue eyes, eyes that looked frightfully familiar, gazed upon me in two second intervals. Her tiny fingers curled around mine and conveyed the message of dependence and security.

I felt the vertigo of reality rush through my adrenalin bathed body. I felt my lungs become inadequate and my knees wanted to buckle. The reality was rushing forth that I was now a part of that great order of Fatherhood! I held my little girl to my chest and I thanked my God for deeming Christy and I worthy of this honor and asked God for protection for my daughter. And I desperately beseeched God to not let me blow it!

Over the next several weeks reality set in and Christy and I started getting used to being parents. On several nights I've just sat and watched Savannah as she slept in peaceful bliss. I wanted her to have a good life with joy, security, contentment and great memories of a childhood spent with her mom and dad. I would wonder as I watched her, what will she look like? What kind of personality will she have? Will she be athletic? How will she like her life as a P.K. who is living her life behind those ever fragile walls of glass?

I've decided to end this book with a chapter that is dedicated towards the parents of ministers kids. I wish to give you some ideas to make you more apt for success, to help you avoid the pitfalls that have been the demise of so many.

As I have become a parent recently, I've spent many hours reflecting on my upbringing. I tried to remember how my parents raised five children in a home that was so fast-paced and a world that was rapidly succumbing to the ravages of Satan. I thought about the family altars and prayer times, the long talks during dinner, the vacations and hunting trips, the board meetings (spankings), and the lectures that went into the wee hours of the night. I asked myself how did my parents produce a daughter that is married to a pastor and loves God deeply? How did they produce three sons, whom all are ordained men of God and try to serve God with their life? What did they do to keep us kids on the right path?

I now wish to give you some ideas based upon the home I grew up in that helped me grow up behind the walls of glass. I will start with some obvious (but commonly undone) ideas that would apply to any parent. I will then become more pointed with my ideas to pertain to those who live life in the ministry.

"The best thing spent on your children is your time."
—Dr. Curtis Hutson

"A family altar would alter many a family."

1. Have a family altar.

It was the practice of my parents to gather us together each night in the living room before bedtime. We would have a lesson which would be followed up by prayer time.

I remember mom and dad would buy Christian story books. These were books that had a theme verse and then a story to illustrate that verse. This was a great tool to help mold our young minds and teach us character as well as fundamental teachings of the Bible. I also learned about all the great Bible stories such as David and Goliath, Jonah and the whale, and Daniel's triumph in the lion's den.

As a child I looked forward to this time because my dad was so good at telling stories that it made those pages of the Bible literally come alive in my young imaginative mind! I could just see it happening on the movie screen in my head.

We would start the prayer time with prayer requests and then prayer would end the family altar. Many times the altar would be preceded by a board game like Yahtzee or Clue or Uno. These are sweet memories for me. This altar would usually take place about 45 minutes before we went to bed.As I got older and on into my teen years we all had different schedules with jobs and sports and activities. It became impossible for us to be consistent with our family altar time, by that time the foundations had been laid and some habits formed that led me to my own personal altar time. *The family altar was a crucial tool in my spiritual development!*

"The family that prays together, stays together."

—traditional

2. Have the right priorities.

"What shall it profit a man if he should gain the whole world and lose his own children?"

In his book, *One Life,* Christian Bernard tells one of the most heart-breaking personal disaster stories I've ever heard. Christian Bernard was the brilliant doctor who performed the world's first human heart transplant. While developing this medical breakthrough he was required to be away from his home for months at a time. He admits that he was so busy and so caught up in what he was doing that he rarely wrote or even called home to his wife and children at home. Here's what he wrote about his homecoming:

"I hadn't written for two months. Yet I was unprepared for her greeting. 'Why did you come?' There was no longer a smile in her eyes . . . 'We gave you up. We decided you were never coming back!' 'We were building valves, aortic valves,' I answered. 'No, you were building a family. That is, you were until you dumped it in my lap', she said bitterly. 'We have ceased to exist for you.'"

While Dr. Bernard had dedicated his whole being to understanding the human heart, ironically, he failed to understand the heart that mattered most, that of his wife and kids! Although he was successful in an important field, he was a failure in the most important field, that of being a husband and a father!

My dear friend, in the pressure of building a great church or mission, don't forget to build your home! *If you lose your home, you will most assuredly lose your ministry.* I was speaking to a good friend who runs a children's home. With tears in his eyes, he said that his son told him, "You loved those kids in the children's home more than you ever loved me!" He went on to say that this broke his heart and made him redirect his priorities.

I was at a conference recently when I was able to hear some of the greatest preachers in America preach. I heard one young pastor who has been blessed with great talent which he has used to build a fantastic church. He said something that caused my ears to perk up. He said, "I love to work at the church, there's no place I'd rather be, I don't take days off. If I stay home my wife puts me to work around the house, that doesn't build my church so I'd rather be at church where my work has eternal value." I'm sure that he's a great worker and a diligent pastor but he also has a young wife and young children. It is my opinion that my children are my most important life work! It will be them, more than my church, who will carry on my legacy. It doesn't have to be either/or! You can build a great church and build a great family but you must have the right priorities.

God told husbands to love their wife as He loved His bride, the church. I've heard many pastor's wives say that their husband had a mistress and that mistress was his ministry! If you are one who has put your ministry first, then you are wrong! You must ask God to forgive you and then ask forgiveness of your family.

Many of the heroes of the faith have paid a huge price. It is said that Dr. Billy Sunday suffered a heart attack when the news that his son died a drunkard's death was delivered to him. In the Bible we see the tragedy of King David and the sword that brought bitter sorrow through his unruly children. We read in I Samuel of how Eli, the high priest was so busy doing the work of God but he forgot to restrain his sons. They were involved in great sin and blasphemy and God killed them both. When Eli was told about their death, he fell off the platform and broke his neck.

Men of God make sure your wife and kids are a priority to you! I guarantee you that years from now the fact that you've been a famous preacher with a huge church and lots of adoring fans will be no comfort to you on those sleepless lonely nights if you lose your family.

3. Be there for important events.

There has been some teachings that have helped form the philosophy of many young pastors that in my opinion have been very damaging to the homes of preachers all across this land. I'm sure that it was done with good intentions to motivate preachers to work harder for the cause of Christ, and not be lazy and waste time. I believe they have been out of balance. Such philosophies as . . .

1. Don't take a day off, the world is going to hell while your fishing or playing golf.
2. Don't take a vacation.
3. Be the first one at the office and the last one to leave. Don't let anyone outwork you!
4. Your schedule is your boss, don't let anyone (including wife and kids) interrupt it.
5. A busy church is a growing church, always have something every night going on at church.

6. Don't let your children even see you without a tie on or shoes on.
7. Church needs to take preeminence over needs of family.
8. Never take your children's side over a family in the church or church staff.

All of these statements I've heard taught by great men of God. I've heard preachers say that they weren't there the day their child was born and have had to be gone on most birthdays since. I've heard of pastors who have church events on every major holiday which keeps them from their families. I've heard preachers brag about how long it's been since they've taken a vacation or a day off. They brag about how many weeks it's been since they've been home or been able to see their kids in sporting events. I've wanted to say, "Shame on you"!! I'm not impressed with your ability to be self absorbed and so out of balance! I'm glad that you've been so successful but it's coming at the expense of the ones you love the most! It won't matter to you that you've led the state in baptisms when your son is arrested for drunkenness! It won't matter to you how many you run in Sunday school when your daughter elopes or has run away from home! You won't care about how famous you are with others when you realize that you are a complete stranger to your own flesh and blood!

We teach our people to be involved with their kids and to know what they are doing. We are painfully aware of the kids at church, the wild ones, the rebellious ones, the ones who need time to be spent with them. However, we are the most surprised when the cold news splashes us in the face that it is our own children who are involved in embarrassing sin! Often it has gone on for years before the parent comes to knowledge of it.

I heard one young man say that his dad cares more for the bus kids than he does his own kids. I heard another young person say that he couldn't remember the last time his dad had dinner with them. I've heard others complain that they believe the ministry is far more important and if it came down between the two, they'd lose.

You must be a diligent worker and minister but don't forget about your family along the way! It won't hurt you to take a day off once in a while to be at home for birthdays, holidays, family reunions, and other events in your family's life.

I promised my wife that I'd be at home for birthdays, anniversaries, holidays and family reunions. I told my church that I would never plan events on holidays that would take them away from their families unless it fell on a regularly scheduled church time. I believe that for us to have strong churches we must have strong families!! You must be at home for important days in your family's life. If you lose your family you will most certainly lose your ministry.

I'm so glad I had a mom and dad who were there for my birthdays, Christmas, Thanksgiving, basketball games and other big days in my life.

4. When your with the family, be with the family.

I've been out with pastors and friends who've spent the whole time on their cell phones or studying books and talking shop. Many ministers make the mistake of always taking others with them on family time. If they go out on a date with their wife, they'll invite another couple every time. If they go on vacation, they'll bring another family with them. I've even heard of preachers taking their family on vacation to week long conferences! You may be with your family but you are not really with them. I'm not saying that it's always wrong to do this but there needs to be family only time in your life. Here are some suggestions to help you accomplish this.

1. Turn the cell phone and beepers off.
2. Instruct your staff that it better be a life or death emergency before they call. (most problems can hang for a day).
3. Don't announce when you'll be gone from your church.
4. Don't announce where you're going until you've returned.
5. Date your wife without others present often .

6. Date your children individually from time to time. (Take them hunting, fishing, shopping, out to eat, picnics, etc.)
7. Don't talk about work the whole time you're together.
8. Avoid lectures or deep topics when on these dates.
9. Plan your time together.
10. Protect your time together.

"Time spent on family is never wasted."

5. Consistency in the home.

"Children disgrace us in public by behaving just like we do at home."

Be sure that you are always practicing what you preach! It will be impossible for your family to respect you as a preacher if they don't respect you as a father! The life you live in public should be the life you live at home as much as possible. Inconsistency is a huge killer of respect. People can over look many things but hypocrisy isn't one of them. Every wise minister is careful when it comes to the watchful eyes of the flock but many are not when it comes to the little eyes at home! Here are some common areas of controversy . . .

1. Mom and Dad's ability to get along.
2. Mother not backing up daddy
   a. Dress standards
   b. Music
   c. Church attendance
   d. Standards
   e. Christian service
   f. Rules of house
3. Skipping church when out of town or on vacation.
4. Movie rentals
5. Cursing
6. Tobacco use
7. Alcohol consumption

8. Laziness
9. Internet chat rooms and porno web sites.
10. Quitting the ministry for periods of time.
11. Consistent discouragement displayed in front of your family. Complaints always go up the chain of command and never down it.
12. Uninforced rules and convictions.

"Parents wonder why the streams are bitter when they themselves have poisoned the fountain."

6. Try to be home for dinner.

In my home dinner was a big time. When we were little, the dinner table was the conference table of our home. Dad tried to be home every day for dinner and mom was a great cook who spent lots of time preparing for this special event each day. In my home there were rules that we lived by to make the dinner table a success.

A. You must be dressed.
B. You must eat at the table and not in front of the T.V.
C. The T.V. was to be turned off.
D. All conversation was to be positive. (No arguing or lectures)
E. If you were at home you must attend.
F. Mom and Dad would ask each one of us about our day.
G. If during that conversation a problem arose it would be discussed privately after dinner.
H. Christian music was often played in the background.
I. Never discuss business at the table.

Use your dinner table to create a tight family with many warm memories!

7. Don't use your office for counseling your family.

It's hard for you to not be a pastor when your in your office. Many P.K.'s say that they feel they only have a pastor and not a dad. It's a good idea to do your discipline and counseling at home or other places. My dad used to take us for a drive when he had serious things to talk to us about. This was wise for several reasons. One.It kept the conversation private. Two. Driving down the road at 60 m.p.h., we couldn't leave, we had to listen! Three. It took my dad out of the "pastor" element and into the "daddy' element.

8. Do not use your kids as examples in the pulpit unless they tell you it's o.k.

This is discussed earlier in the book.

9. Don't keep your kids in the dark about church problems.

As your children become older they should be informed more about church problems because it involves their life too. They can pray, make stands, and feel like part of the team with you more if they know about it, instead of finding out when you're fired or at the next business meeting!

10. Listen to others who inform you of your children's actions.

Some people are malicious but most people are sincerely trying to be helpful when they tell on your kids. If several people all say that your child has done something then most likely it is true. Give your child a chance to explain his side of it but when the evidence is there of his guilt, don't be blind! No one likes a prima donna and your child will be resented for it.

I was at camp several years ago when I was informed that a pastor's son was caught sneaking out of the cabin with the intent to meet a girl in the woods. This young man was known for his rebellion and had been trouble all week long. When I met with him and his dad, his dad exploded! He got mad at his son, at me and at the other staff who were involved! He viewed it as a personal attack and he went on to say to his son that because of you no one will ask me to preach in revivals and conferences or special meetings. He was going to load all of his church group and go home right then and there. His wife calmed him down but the result has been this, he's never came back to camp and he has nothing to do with me at all.

We were just trying to help him and enforce some common sense rules but he had a deaf ear when it came to his children. He's not listened to anyone who has tried to help him. He, sadly, has had many problems in his home over the years. Not everyone who tells on your kids is out to harm them. Be wise.

11. Involve your children in the work of God.

This is discussed earlier in the book.

12. Expose your children to men of God.

I was privileged to get to be around some great men of God as I was growing up, to hear their stories and words of wisdom, to see them as real people with great hearts. I could feel the power of God on them as they spoke. It was my dad's practice to always have at least one meal that was reserved for us kids and mom to have with the guest speaker. We would get to know them as friends and heroes. I'll never forget hearing Dr. Jim Vinyard tell of his Vietnam stories and hunting stories. The hair on the back of my neck would stand up! I've talked about football with Dr. Jack Hyles and racquetball with Dr. Russell Anderson. I've laughed until I thought I would die while hearing Dr. Johnny Pope tell jokes at the restaurant with my family as his private audience. These are great times and memories for me. I'm glad that my mom and dad exposed me to such great men.

13. Dress sharp.

I see so many parents who look like fashion misfits! The way they dress in clothes from 20 years ago is an embarrassment to their children. My mom and dad were great examples to me in this area. My mom was described many times as "looking like she just stepped out of a fashion magazine." I was always proud of my parents and one reason was that they looked good! They had class and style that brought dignity to our family.

14. Don't run down other preachers to your kids.

15. Tell your kids you love them every day!

16. Be affectionate with your wife in front of your kids often.

> *"One of the best things a father can do for his children is to demonstrate an obvious love for their mother."*
>
> —Dr. Curtis Hutson

17. Forgive and forget.

You must be able to convey to your children that they are forgiven and that they are still loved. They must know that you are still proud of them even though you've had to discipline them. Don't keep a reminder of all their troubles handy to throw up at them every time they get into trouble. If they ever feel that you've lost hope in them then they will cease to try.

18. Be happy.

A happy home is a home where kids wish to be. When you walk in the door do all you can to be up and a joy for your family. Leave the pressures on the doorstep and enjoy the home that God has given you! Sadly, many P.K.'s only remember parents who were stressed out, discouraged, angry and tired.

> *"The spirit of a man will sustain his infirmity; but a wounded spirit who can bear?"*
>
> —Proverbs 18:14

19. Teach them about their Christian heritage.

It is a great way to instill pride and for them to form an identity. Tell them of the great price paid by Christianity over the years and the sacrifices made by millions for the cause of Christ. Also tell them about the ministries of John Bunyan, the Apostles and modern day people who've made great stands for the Bible and our Saviour. Your children will develop pride and see the importance of your beliefs. Teach them who and what they are.

20. Have an "Open door" policy with your kids.

I heard one pastor's son say that in order for him to see his dad he had to schedule it with his dad's secretary. If he just popped in he wouldn't get but a few moments with his dad. I feel that this is a crazy notion. If my wife calls and I'm in a meeting she knows that if she needs me, my secretary will break in and get me. I always know my dad would rearrange his schedule to see me if I needed him. Your wife and kids need to know that they have V.I.P. access to you at any time!

These are just some of the things that my parents did to help us kids make it through our life behind walls of glass.

❖ ❖ ❖ ❖ ❖ ❖ ❖ ❖ ❖

A Father's Prayer

By Douglas McArthur

Build me a son, O Lord, who will be strong enough to know when he is weak, and brave enough to face himself when he is afraid; one who will be proud and unbending in honest defeat, humble and gentle in victory.

Build me a son whose wishbone will not be where his backbone should be; a son who will know Thee and that to know himself is the foundation stone of knowledge.

Lead him, I pray, not in the path of ease and comfort, but under the stress and spur of difficulties and challenge. Here let him learn to stand up in the storm; here let him learn compassion for those who fail.

Build me a son whose heart will be clear, whose goal will be high; a son who will master himself before he seeks to master other men; one who will learn to laugh, yet never forget how to weep; one who will reach into the future, yet never forget the past.

And after all these things are his, add, I pray, enough of a sense of humor so that he may always be serious, yet never take himself too seriously. Give him humility, so that he may always remember the simplicity of true greatness, the open mind of true wisdom, the meekness of true strength.

Then I, his father, will dare to whisper, "I have not lived in vain."

* * * * * * * *

A Father's Prayer
By Douglas MacArthur

